TACOS & TEQUILA

TACOS & TEQUILA

13-Digit ISBN: 978-1-40034-076-7
10-Digit ISBN: 1-40034-076-4

This book may be ordered by mail from the publisher.
Please include $5.99 for postage and handling.

Please support your local bookseller first!

Books published by Cider Mill Press Book Publishers are available at special discounts for bulk purchases in the United States by corporations, institutions, and other organizations. For more information, please contact the publisher.

Cider Mill Press Book Publishers
"Where good books are ready for press"
501 Nelson Place
Nashville, Tennessee 37214

cidermillpress.com

Typography: Acumin Pro, Ballinger, Kiln, Lulo

Printed in Malaysia

Image Credits: Pages 18, 61, 69, 77, 82, 103, 111, 115, 118–119, 120, 125, 134–135, 137, 138, 142, 194, 197, 198, 201, 205, 206, 209, 218, 221, and 229 courtesy of Cider Mill Press. All other images and vectors used under official license from Shutterstock.com.

24 25 26 27 28 OFF 5 4 3 2 1
First Edition

TACOS & TEQUILA

100+ VIBRANT RECIPES THAT BRING MEXICO TO YOUR KITCHEN

CIDER MILL PRESS

BOOK PUBLISHERS

CONTENTS

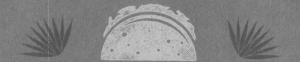

INTRODUCTION

As we all know, the taco is a perfect dish, one of those rare foods that becomes so beloved that people come to identify it with a specific day of the week, and spend every other day eagerly awaiting its return to the table.

But the true believers know that tacos are too good, and too versatile to restrict to just one meal on a specific weekday or weeknight. Indeed, tacos can serve as the centerpiece of a weekend dinner party (and turn such a gathering into one that is far more enjoyable and relaxed than is typical), provide almost-instant comfort on those evenings when the world has worn you down, and serve as the perfect landing spot for any leftovers and odds and ends that you have in your refrigerator and pantry.

While a taco is capable of rising to meet any charge, it can only do so if its foundation—the tortilla—is in the right place. And while store-bought options are continually getting better, taco connoisseurs know that there is nothing that can compare to the pleasure of a taco built upon a well-made homemade tortilla. Simply put, the tortilla is not just there as a wrapper for your filling and fixings—instead, it is there to provide the texture and flavor that can enhance the other elements present.

Once you have your bases squared away, there are essentially an infinite number of options available to you. You can keep it classic and go with a perfectly seasoned ground beef taco, or the lightly fried fish tacos that have gradually migrated away from their birthplace—Baja, Mexico—and taken over menus across the globe. You can use the taco's unsurpassed versatility to encase one of the clever innovations the contemporary culinary revolution has fashioned, or some flavorful preparation that suits your particular dietary preferences.

Once you've made that decision, all that's left is putting the finishing touches on your masterpiece, and applying whichever fixings go best, or please your unique palate.

When the tacos are ready to go, we recognize that such a momentous occasion calls for a cocktail—one centered around tequila and/or mezcal. Accordingly, we've gathered everything from classics like the Margarita and laid-back long sippers like the Paloma to innovative and elegant serves from some of the world's best bars. It's a collection of drinks that is sure to help you to capture the desired vibe, and make each and every taco night something memorable.

A BRIEF OVERVIEW OF TEQUILA & MEZCAL

For starters, all tequila is mezcal. But not all mezcal is tequila. Those of you who are confused, think of it this way: all bourbon is whiskey, but not all whiskey is bourbon.

Both tequila and mezcal are made by distilling the core of the agave plant, known as the piña. There are about 30 different varietals of agave plant that can be used to make mezcals. Only blue agave can be used to produce tequila.

Tequila and mezcal come from different regions of Mexico. Tequila makers can be found in the northern and central parts of the country—Michoacán, Guanajuato, Nayarit, Tamaulipas, and Jalisco, which is where the town of Tequila is located. Oaxaca, which is in southern Mexico, is where 85 percent of mezcal is produced, though it is also made in Durango, Guanajuato, Guerrero, San Luis Potosí, Tamaulipas, Zacatecas, Michoacán, and Puebla.

The separation between the two spirits, in the global imagination, began with Mexico's victory in 1810's War of Independence. Fueled by the energy of that unexpected triumph, those in charge of the burgeoning republic began to look to an increasingly industrialized Europe for inspiration. In Tequila, mezcal producers started to shake off the yoke of the hacienda system, gaining the ability to acquire more capital—resources they had the wisdom to reinvest into their operations. Eventually, Martin Martinez de Castro introduced the copper column still to the town. This innovation, when combined with the development of cooking the agave in a stone oven instead of the traditional earthen pit, bolstered production immensely.

From there, it was little more than a numbers game. Tequila, through sheer quantity and market share, became embedded in most people's minds as Mexico's spirit. And mezcal, by remaining tied to the craft culture that had fostered it, came—until very recently—to be seen as an altogether separate category, a curiosity surrounded by myth and misunderstanding.

To make tequila, the agave is steamed in ovens before being distilled in copper stills. Once distilled, it is aged in oak barrels, and the amount of time spent in the barrel determines the type of tequila that is bottled. A breakdown of the various types follows:

PLATA (NO MORE THAN 2 MONTHS)

Also called blanco, silver, joven, or white tequila, this is the purest form of distilled blue agave. Once it has been distilled, it is quickly bottled and distributed. Plata should taste fresh and fruity, with a clean, herbaceous hint. The best way to imbibe plata is on the rocks with a squeeze of fresh lime.

REPOSADO (2 TO 12 MONTHS)

Extra time in the barrel lets this "rested" tequila mellow out, and imparts a hint of flavors, ranging from oak to vanilla, baking spices, and fruit.

AÑEJO (1 TO 3 YEARS)

This tequila has more depth and complexity than both plata and reposado, featuring notes of wood, nuts, and chocolate. While each brand is unique in terms of wood used and resting time, all añejo is going to be soft, smooth, and distinct on the palate.

EXTRA AÑEJO (MINIMUM OF 3 YEARS)

This "extra aged" variety is a relative newcomer to the scene, only becoming an official classification in March 2006.

Tequila, like Champagne, is a designated Appellation of Origin (AO). Like all mezcal, the agave used to produce tequila is tended to by individuals known as jimadors, who still largely perform their work by hand. In order to get a product that is saleable, these jimadors have to plant the agave, care for the plants, and harvest them when they are perfectly ripe. A huge amount of time, energy, and passion gets put into every bottle of pure blue agave tequila. That's even more the case when the tequila is aged.

If you've noticed the continual appearance of "pure" in reference to tequila, that is not an accident. Most everyone knows someone who has tequila firmly on their personal no-fly list. This is undoubtedly due to an encounter with a tequila that was less than 100 percent blue agave, or a mixto. Since they are cheaper to produce, there are many more mixto brands on the market than there are pure agave brands. Legally, these mixto tequilas must be made with at least 51 percent pure blue agave sugar. The other portion of the sugars can be from non-agave sources, like sugarcane, which will affect the taste of the spirit in a negative fashion, and potentially make the aftereffects of an evening much worse. So, in order to make sure you're getting the best experience, carefully read the label of any tequila bottle before you purchase, and say no to mixtos.

To produce mezcal, the agave is cooked over charcoal in basalt-lined pits dug in the ground, and distillation happens in clay vessels; this is why most mezcals have a smoky flavor, though, as with Scotch, there are exceptions, with some offerings featuring no smoke at all, and others just a trace to provide balance. Like tequila, mezcal is aged in oak barrels.

Until recently, most people outside of Mexico marked mezcal as "the one with the worm." The existence of this meme appears to be tied to a popular marketing campaign put forth by the Monte Alban brand during the '70s. The worm, or gusano, appeared in every bottle of Monte Alban, but it is not a hallmark of the spirit, as many believed it to be. Though it does still pop up from time to time. The gusano, which feeds upon the agave plant, is believed to be highly nutritious. It can be consumed on its own, or dropped into a bottle, where it does everything from hide unpleasant flavors to add a subtle, pleasant fungal note to a well-crafted mezcal.

Mezcal, due to its association with the rural South and the folk cultures that prevail there, was also misunderstood within Mexico for a long period of time. This began to change when a growing appreciation for craft and heritage entered the national mindset, shifting mezcal from an easily dismissed oddity to a powerfully deep tradition that shifts as one moves from village to village. This rich provincialism contributed much to the lore that surrounds mezcal, including the claim that it will cause those who imbibe to hallucinate. While that is not the case, there is a school that believes the agave sugars in mezcal do produce a stimulating and energizing effect that causes a slightly higher degree of awareness than that which is employed in everyday life.

When selecting a mezcal, much can be determined by looking at the percentage of alcohol. Simply put, the higher the ABV, the less watered down the product is, and the more oils the distillate will contain. These oils provide the spirit with rich flavors and complexity, which is appealing to the aficionado, less so to the entrepreneur looking for global appeal, as they are after a cleaner tasting product with less variance. A good rule of thumb: anything at 40 percent ABV is made for a foreign market, though some of these offerings are designated as "single village," meaning they will carry a distinctive character. Anything at 46 percent and up can be trusted to carry the taste of a traditional mezcal.

TACOS

The versatility of tacos is a large part of what has made them a global sensation that millions of people gladly build their week around. At one moment, they can be the ultimate comfort food. In another, they can provide the foundation for a lively yet elegant dinner party.

Able to accommodate every whim and bit of intuition, the taco is a true wonder, bouncing happily between cultures and cuisines, welcoming to all. Rest assured, the recipes in this chapter are only the beginning of your encounters with the unsurpassed adaptability of the taco.

YIELD:
32 TORTILLAS

ACTIVE TIME:
45 MINUTES

TOTAL TIME:
45 MINUTES

CORN TORTILLAS

1 lb. masa harina

1½ tablespoons kosher salt

3 cups warm filtered water, plus more as needed

1   In the work bowl of a stand mixer fitted with the paddle attachment, combine the masa harina and salt. With the mixer on low speed, slowly begin to add the water. The mixture should come together as a soft, smooth dough. You want the masa to be moist enough so that when a small ball of it is pressed flat in your hands, the edges do not crack. Also, it should not stick to your hands when you peel it off your palm.

2   Let the masa rest for 10 minutes and check the hydration again. You may need to add more water, depending on environmental conditions.

3   Warm a cast-iron skillet over high heat. Portion the masa into 1-ounce balls and cover them with a damp linen towel.

4   Line a tortilla press with two 8-inch circles of plastic. You can use a grocery store bag, a resealable bag, or even a standard kitchen trash bag as a source for the plastic. Place a masa ball in the center of one circle and gently push down on it with the palm of one hand to flatten. Place the other plastic circle on top and then close the tortilla press, applying firm, even pressure to flatten the masa into a round tortilla.

5   Open the tortilla press and remove the top layer of plastic. Carefully pick up the tortilla and remove the bottom piece of plastic.

6   Gently lay the tortilla flat in the pan, taking care to not wrinkle it. Cook for 15 to 30 seconds, until the edge begins to lift up slightly. Turn the tortilla over and let it cook for 30 to 45 seconds before turning it over one last time. If the hydration of the masa is correct and the heat is high enough, the tortilla should puff up and inflate. Remove the tortilla from the pan and store in a tortilla warmer lined with a linen towel. Repeat until all of the prepared masa has been made into tortillas.

YIELD:
18 TORTILLAS

ACTIVE TIME:
45 MINUTES

TOTAL TIME:
1 HOUR AND 30 MINUTES

FLOUR TORTILLAS

1 lb. all-purpose flour, plus more as needed

1 tablespoon kosher salt

1 tablespoon baking powder

2½ oz. lard or unsalted butter, melted

1 to 1¼ cups warm filtered water (105°F)

1 In the work bowl of a stand mixer fitted with the paddle attachment, combine the flour, salt, and baking powder and beat on low speed for 30 seconds.

2 Gradually add the lard and beat until the mixture is a coarse meal.

3 Fit the mixer with the dough hook and set it to low speed. Add the water in a slow stream until the dough begins to come together, 2 to 3 minutes. The dough should begin to pull away from the side of the mixing bowl, leaving no residue behind. Increase the speed to medium and continue mixing until the dough becomes very soft, shiny, and elastic. Please note that more or less of the water may be required due to environmental conditions and/or variations in the flour.

4 Remove the dough from the work bowl and place it in a mixing bowl. Cover with plastic wrap or a damp kitchen towel and let it rest at room temperature for 30 to 45 minutes.

5 Portion the dough into rounds the size of golf balls, approximately 1½ oz. each. Using the palms of your hands, roll the rounds in a circular motion until they are seamless balls. Place them on a parchment-lined baking sheet and cover with plastic wrap. Let them rest at room temperature for 20 minutes.

6 Working on a very smooth and flour-dusted work surface, roll out the balls of dough until they are between ⅛ and ¼ inch thick and about 8 inches in diameter. Stack the tortillas, separating each one with pieces of parchment paper that have been cut to size.

7 Warm a cast-iron skillet over medium-high heat. Gently place a tortilla in the pan. It should immediately sizzle and start to puff up. Do not puncture it. Cook, turning frequently, for 20 to 30 seconds per side, until the tortilla is lightly golden brown in spots. Place in a linen towel, a tortilla warmer, or a plastic resealable bag so it continues to steam and repeat with the remaining tortillas.

TACOS

19

YIELD:
4 SERVINGS

ACTIVE TIME:
30 MINUTES

TOTAL TIME:
2 HOURS AND 30 MINUTES

CHICKEN TACOS

1 yellow onion, chopped

10 garlic cloves, trimmed

2 scotch bonnet chile peppers, stems and seeds removed, chopped

1 cup fresh cilantro, chopped

1 teaspoon dried thyme

1 tablespoon cumin

½ teaspoon allspice

1 cup orange juice

½ cup fresh lemon juice

½ teaspoon citric acid

Zest and juice of 1 lime

¼ cup extra-virgin olive oil

Salt and pepper, to taste

2 lbs. boneless, skinless chicken breasts

Tortillas, for serving

1   Place all of the ingredients, except for the chicken and tortillas, in a food processor or blender and puree until smooth. Pour the marinade into a large resealable plastic bag, and add the chicken. Place in the refrigerator and marinate for 2 hours. If time allows, let the chicken marinate for up to 8 hours.

2   Prepare a gas or charcoal grill for medium-high heat (about 450°F). Remove the chicken from the refrigerator, remove it from the marinade, and pat it dry.

3   Place the chicken on the grill and cook until both sides are charred and the breasts are cooked through and springy to the touch, 4 to 5 minutes per side. Transfer the chicken to a plate, tent it with aluminum foil, and let it rest for 10 minutes.

4   While the chicken is resting, place the reserved marinade in a saucepan and bring to a simmer over medium heat, until it starts to thicken, about 10 minutes. Spoon it over the chicken and serve with tortillas and your favorite taco fixings.

YIELD:
4 SERVINGS

ACTIVE TIME:
15 MINUTES

TOTAL TIME:
20 MINUTES

BEEF TACOS

1 tablespoon extra-virgin olive oil, plus more as needed

1 lb. ground beef

1 tablespoon kosher salt

2 teaspoons cumin

2 teaspoons paprika

1 tablespoon garlic powder

1 teaspoon cayenne pepper

1 teaspoon chili powder

Tortillas, for serving

1   Place the olive oil in a large skillet and warm it over medium-high heat.

2   Add the ground beef and all of the seasonings. Cook, breaking up the meat with a wooden spoon, until it is browned and cooked through, about 8 minutes.

3   Serve with tortillas and your favorite taco fixings.

BEEF TACOS, SEE PAGE 21

YIELD:
4 SERVINGS

ACTIVE TIME:
25 MINUTES

TOTAL TIME:
24 HOURS

BLACKENED SALMON TACOS

1½ tablespoons paprika

1 tablespoon chili powder

1 tablespoon cumin

1½ teaspoons coriander

½ teaspoon cayenne pepper

1 tablespoon onion powder

2 teaspoons garlic powder

2 teaspoons black pepper

2 teaspoons kosher salt

2 tablespoons avocado oil

2 lbs. salmon fillets, skin removed

Tortillas, for serving

1   Preheat the oven to 450°F. Place all of the seasonings in a bowl, stir to combine, and set the blackening spice mixture aside.

2   Place the avocado oil in a large cast-iron skillet and warm it over medium-high heat. Dredge the salmon in the blackening spice mixture and then carefully place the salmon in the skillet. Sear on each side for 1 minute.

3   Transfer the pan to the oven and roast the salmon until the internal temperature of each piece is 135°F, 3 to 4 minutes.

4   Remove the salmon from the oven and let it rest for 5 minutes. Chop the salmon and serve it with tortillas and your favorite taco fixings.

YIELD:
4 SERVINGS

ACTIVE TIME:
30 MINUTES

TOTAL TIME:
1 HOUR

BAJA FISH TACOS

2 lbs. tilapia fillets, quartered

½ teaspoon kosher salt, plus more to taste

Black pepper, to taste

1 lb. masa harina

¾ cup water, plus more as needed

Canola oil, as needed

Tortillas, for serving

1   Season the tilapia with salt and pepper.

2   Place the masa in a baking dish, add the salt, and then the water. Stir to combine. Stick a wooden spoon into the batter; you want it to coat the spoon and drip slowly off. Depending on the brand of masa used, you may need to add more water to get the proper consistency.

3   Dredge the tilapia in the masa mixture until it is evenly coated.

4   Add canola oil to a Dutch oven until it is 2 inches deep and warm it to 350°F.

5   Working in batches to avoid crowding the pot, gently slip the tilapia into the hot oil. Fry the tilapia until it is cooked through, golden brown, and crispy, 8 to 10 minutes.

6   Remove the fried tilapia from the hot oil and transfer it to a paper towel–lined plate to drain.

7   Chop the tilapia into bite-size pieces and serve with tortillas and your favorite taco fixings.

BAJA FISH TACOS, SEE PAGE 25

YIELD:
6 SERVINGS

ACTIVE TIME:
20 MINUTES

TOTAL TIME:
1 HOUR AND 20 MINUTES

CHICKEN TINGA TACOS

2 bone-in, skin-on chicken legs

2 bone-in, skin-on chicken thighs

2 tablespoons kosher salt, plus more to taste

2 bay leaves

1 tablespoon extra-virgin olive oil

1 white onion, sliced thin

1 garlic clove, sliced thin

3 large tomatoes, diced

2 chipotle chile peppers, stems and seeds removed

Tortillas, for serving

1   Place the chicken in a large pot and cover it with cold water by at least an inch. Add the salt and bay leaves and bring the water to a simmer. Cook the chicken until the meat pulls away from the bones, about 40 minutes.

2   While the chicken is simmering, place the olive oil in a large skillet and warm it over medium heat. Add the onion and garlic and cook, stirring frequently, until the onion is translucent, about 3 minutes. Reduce the heat to low and cook until the onion has softened.

3   Add the diced tomatoes and cook for another 5 minutes. Remove the pan from heat.

4   Remove the chicken from the pot and shred it with 2 forks. Reserve 2 cups of the cooking liquid. Place the chiles in a bowl with 1 cup of the cooking liquid and let them sit until tender, about 20 minutes.

5   Chop the chiles, add them to the skillet along with the shredded chicken, and cook over medium heat, stirring occasionally, until the flavor has developed to your liking, about 8 minutes. Add the remaining cooking liquid to the pan if it becomes too dry.

6   Season the dish with salt and serve with tortillas and your favorite taco fixings.

YIELD:
6 SERVINGS

ACTIVE TIME:
25 MINUTES

TOTAL TIME:
1 HOUR AND 25 MINUTES

PORK RIB TACOS

Salt, to taste

4 lbs. pork ribs, cut into 3-inch-wide pieces

1 white onion

4 garlic cloves

2 bay leaves

4 guajillo chile peppers, stems and seeds removed

2 pasilla chile peppers, stems and seeds removed

4 chipotle mortia chile peppers, stems and seeds removed

2 tablespoons cumin seeds

1 tablespoon dried thyme

½ cup lard or extra-virgin olive oil

Tortillas, for serving

1   Fill a large saucepan with water, season it generously with salt, add the ribs, onion, garlic, and bay leaves, and bring the water to a boil. Reduce the heat to medium and cook until the ribs are tender but not falling apart, about 1 hour.

2   Place the chile peppers in a dry skillet and toast over medium heat until they darken and become fragrant and pliable. Transfer them to a bowl of hot water and let them soak for 20 minutes.

3   Place the cumin seeds in the dry skillet and toast until they are fragrant, shaking the pan frequently. Transfer the toasted seeds to a small dish.

4   Drain the chiles, place them in a blender, and add the thyme, toasted cumin seeds, onion, garlic, and 2 cups of the cooking liquid. Puree until smooth, taste the puree, and season it with salt.

5   When the ribs are tender, remove them from the pan and set them on paper towels to drain.

6   Place the lard in a large, deep skillet and warm it over medium heat. Add the ribs and sear until they are browned all over, turning them as necessary.

7   Drain any excess fat from the pan, strain the puree over the ribs, and cook over low heat for 10 minutes.

8   Serve with tortillas and your favorite taco fixings.

YIELD:
6 SERVINGS

ACTIVE TIME:
15 MINUTES

TOTAL TIME:
2 HOURS AND 15 MINUTES

CARNITAS TACOS

4 lbs. pork shoulder, cut into 3-inch cubes

Salt and pepper, to taste

1 tablespoon cumin

1 cup lard

1 onion, quartered

1 head of garlic, halved at the equator

Juice of 2 oranges

1 cinnamon stick

1 (12 oz.) can of cola

Tortillas, for serving

1   Season the pork with salt, pepper, and the cumin. Place the lard in a Dutch oven and warm it over medium-high heat. Add the pork, onion, garlic, orange juice, and cinnamon stick and cook until the pork is very tender and well browned, about 1½ hours. Adjust the heat as necessary to ensure it doesn't brown too quickly.

2   Preheat the oven to 400°F and place a wire rack in a rimmed baking sheet. When the pork is very tender, add the cola to the Dutch oven and cook for about 10 minutes.

3   Remove the pork from the pot and place it on the wire rack. Place the pork in the oven and roast it until the outside is crispy, 10 to 20 minutes.

4   Remove the carnitas from the oven and serve it with tortillas and your favorite taco fixings.

CARNITAS TACOS, SEE PAGE 31

YIELD:
4 SERVINGS

ACTIVE TIME:
15 MINUTES

TOTAL TIME:
15 MINUTES

CHORIZO TACOS

2 tablespoons avocado oil

1 lb. chorizo, casing removed

Tortillas, for serving

1   Place the avocado oil in a large skillet and warm it over medium heat.

2   Add the chorizo and cook until it is browned all over and cooked through, 6 to 8 minutes, breaking it up with a wooden spoon as it cooks.

3   Remove the chorizo with a slotted spoon and serve it with tortillas and your favorite taco fixings.

YIELD:
4 SERVINGS

ACTIVE TIME:
20 MINUTES

TOTAL TIME:
4 HOURS AND 30 MINUTES

BBQ CHICKEN TACOS

1¼ cups ketchup

1 cup dark brown sugar

¼ cup molasses

¼ cup apple cider vinegar

¼ cup water

1 tablespoon Worcestershire sauce

2 teaspoons mustard powder

2 teaspoons garlic powder

2 teaspoons smoked paprika

¼ teaspoon cayenne pepper

Salt and pepper, to taste

1 tablespoon all-purpose flour

1½ lbs. boneless, skinless chicken thighs

Tortillas, for serving

1   Place all of the ingredients, except for the flour, chicken, and tortillas, in a saucepan and stir to combine. Bring the sauce to a boil over medium-high heat.

2   Reduce the heat to medium and cook the sauce until it has reduced by one-third, about 20 minutes.

3   Gradually add the flour to the sauce, stirring continually to prevent lumps from forming.

4   Simmer the sauce for another 5 minutes, taste, and adjust the seasoning as necessary.

5   Place the chicken in a slow cooker and pour the sauce over it. Cook on low until the chicken is tender and cooked through, about 4 hours.

6   Remove the chicken from the slow cooker, shred it with forks, and serve with tortillas and your favorite taco fixings.

YIELD:
8 SERVINGS

ACTIVE TIME:
2 HOURS

TOTAL TIME:
12 HOURS

BBQ BRISKET TACOS

5 lbs. center-cut beef brisket

½ cup paprika

6 tablespoons black pepper

2 tablespoons chipotle chile powder

2 tablespoons chili powder

4 teaspoons cayenne pepper

2 teaspoons cumin

2 teaspoons dried oregano

1 tablespoon kosher salt

2 tablespoons extra-virgin olive oil

Tortillas, for serving

1   Trim any fatty areas on the brisket so that the fat is within approximately ¼ inch of the meat, keeping in mind that it is better to leave too much fat than too little.

2   Place the paprika, black pepper, chipotle powder, chili powder, cayenne, cumin, oregano, and salt in a mixing bowl and stir to combine.

3   Rub the brisket with the olive oil and then generously apply the rub, making sure to knead it into the meat. Cover the brisket with plastic wrap and chill it in the refrigerator for 2 hours.

4   Prepare a gas or charcoal grill for low heat (225°F to 250°F).

5   Wrap the brisket in aluminum foil and place it on the grill. Cook until the brisket is very tender and the interior temperature is 190°F to 200°F, 6 to 10 hours.

6   Remove the brisket from heat and let it rest for 20 to 30 minutes before slicing and serving it with tortillas and your favorite taco fixings.

YIELD:
4 SERVINGS

ACTIVE TIME:
20 MINUTES

TOTAL TIME:
20 MINUTES

QUESO BIRRIA TACOS

**4 Corn Tortillas
(see page 16)**

**4 oz. Monterey jack cheese,
shredded**

**1 lb. beef from Birria
(see page 237)**

1 cup warm Birria broth

1 Place the tortillas in a large cast-iron skillet and warm them for 30 seconds on each side.

2 Distribute the cheese over the tortillas and cook until it starts to melt.

3 Top the cheese with some of the beef and fold the tortillas over to make tacos. Cook for 20 seconds, flip the tacos over, and cook for another 20 seconds.

4 Divide the broth among 4 cups and serve it alongside your favorite taco fixings.

QUESO BIRRIA TACOS, SEE PAGE 39

YIELD:
4 SERVINGS

ACTIVE TIME:
30 MINUTES

TOTAL TIME:
2 HOURS AND 30 MINUTES

CARNE ASADA TACOS

1 jalapeño chile pepper, stem and seeds removed, minced

3 garlic cloves, minced

½ cup chopped fresh cilantro

¼ cup avocado oil

Juice of 1 orange

2 tablespoons apple cider vinegar

2 teaspoons cayenne pepper

1 teaspoon ancho chile powder

1 teaspoon garlic powder

1 teaspoon paprika

1 teaspoon kosher salt

1 teaspoon cumin

1 teaspoon dried oregano

¼ teaspoon black pepper

2 lbs. flank steak, trimmed

Tortillas, for serving

1   Place all of the ingredients, except for the steak and tortillas, in a large resealable plastic bag and stir to combine. Add the steak, place the bag in the refrigerator, and let the steak marinate for 2 hours.

2   Prepare a gas or charcoal grill for medium-high heat (about 450°F). Remove the steak from the marinade, pat it dry, and let it rest at room temperature.

3   Place the steak on the grill and cook until it is medium-rare (the interior registers 130°F on an instant-read thermometer) and the exterior is nicely seared, 6 to 8 minutes, turning it over just once.

4   Remove the steak from heat and let it rest for 2 minutes before slicing it thin against the grain and serving it with tortillas and your favorite taco fixings.

YIELD:
4 SERVINGS

ACTIVE TIME:
10 MINUTES

TOTAL TIME:
35 MINUTES

PICADILLO TACOS

2 tablespoons extra-virgin olive oil

2 lbs. ground beef

Salt, to taste

1 teaspoon cumin

1½ teaspoons dried oregano

1½ teaspoons chili powder

1 tablespoon tomato paste

1 onion, finely diced

2 serrano chile peppers, stems and seeds removed, chopped

2 bay leaves

1 lb. Yukon Gold potatoes, peeled and diced

½ lb. carrots, peeled and finely diced

3 large tomatoes, finely diced

½ cup peas

Tortillas, for serving

1   Place the olive oil in a large skillet and warm it over medium heat. Add the ground beef, season it with salt, and cook, breaking the meat up with a wooden spoon, until it is browned, about 6 minutes.

2   Stir in the cumin, oregano, and chili powder, cook for 1 minute, and then stir in the tomato paste, onion, and peppers. Cook until the onion has softened, about 5 minutes.

3   Add the bay leaves, potatoes, carrots, and tomatoes and cook until the potatoes are tender and the flavors have developed to your liking, about 20 minutes. Add the peas when the potatoes have about 5 minutes left to cook.

4   Serve with tortillas and your favorite taco fixings.

YIELD:
8 SERVINGS

ACTIVE TIME:
10 MINUTES

TOTAL TIME:
2 HOURS AND 10 MINUTES

PULLED PORK TACOS

6 lbs. pork shoulder, cut into 5-inch chunks

1 head of garlic, halved at the equator

1 onion, quartered

2 bay leaves

5 sprigs of fresh thyme

4 oz. salt

10 cups water

5 cups BBQ sauce (see page 36 for homemade)

Tortillas, for serving

1   Preheat the oven to 365°F. Place all of the ingredients, except for the tortillas, in a large roasting pan and bring it to a simmer over medium heat. Cook for 10 minutes.

2   Cover the roasting pan with aluminum foil, place it in the oven, and cook until the pork is very tender, about 2 hours.

3   Remove the pork from the oven, shred it with two forks, and serve it with tortillas and your favorite taco fixings.

YIELD:
4 SERVINGS

ACTIVE TIME:
30 MINUTES

TOTAL TIME:
1½ TO 2½ HOURS

DZIK DE RES TACOS

2 lbs. beef brisket

Salt, to taste

8 cups Beef Stock (see page 238)

3 garlic cloves

2 bay leaves

4 sprigs of fresh thyme

½ onion, charred

½ cinnamon stick

1 teaspoon dried oregano

1 teaspoon chopped fresh marjoram

1 cup fresh lime juice

1 cup orange juice

3 oz. radishes, sliced thin

3 habanero chile peppers, stems and seeds removed, minced

1 large red onion, julienned

Flesh of 2 avocados, sliced

½ lb. Roma tomatoes, seeded and finely diced

Tortillas, for serving

1   Trim any fatty areas on the brisket so that the fat is within approximately ¼ inch of the meat, keeping in mind that it is better to leave too much fat than too little. Cut the brisket into 4 pieces.

2   Season the brisket with salt and place it in a large saucepan with the stock. Bring to a simmer over medium heat.

3   Using a piece of cheesecloth, create a sachet with the garlic, bay leaves, thyme, onion, cinnamon stick, oregano, and marjoram. Secure the sachet with kitchen twine and add it to the saucepan.

4   Simmer the brisket until it is very tender, 1 to 2 hours. If time allows, let the meat cool in the broth.

5   Strain the liquid and reserve it for another preparation. Shred the brisket into thin strands, place them in a mixing bowl, add the lime juice and orange juice, and stir to combine. Season with salt and then fold in the radishes, habanero, red onion, avocados, and tomatoes.

6   Serve with tortillas and your favorite taco fixings.

YIELD:
6 SERVINGS

ACTIVE TIME:
20 MINUTES

TOTAL TIME:
1 HOUR AND 20 MINUTES

JERK CHICKEN TACOS

1 tablespoon allspice

1 teaspoon ground cloves

½ teaspoon cinnamon

1 teaspoon cumin

1 tablespoon sugar

1 bunch of fresh cilantro

Juice of 3 limes

Juice of 1 orange

3 habanero chile peppers, stems and seeds removed

1 tablespoon kosher salt

1 cup extra-virgin olive oil

3 to 4 lbs. boneless, skinless chicken pieces

Tortillas, for serving

1   Place all of the ingredients, except for the olive oil, chicken, and tortillas, in a blender and puree until smooth. With the blender running, slowly drizzle in the olive oil until it has emulsified.

2   Place the chicken in a baking dish, pour the marinade over it, and let it marinate in the refrigerator for 1 hour.

3   Prepare a gas or charcoal grill for medium-high heat (about 450°F). Place the chicken on the grill and cook until it is charred and the interior is 165°F, turning it as necessary.

4   Remove the chicken from the grill and let it rest for 10 minutes before chopping it. Serve with tortillas and your favorite taco fixings.

JERK CHICKEN TACOS, SEE PAGE 49

YIELD:
4 SERVINGS

ACTIVE TIME:
15 MINUTES

TOTAL TIME:
5 TO 7 HOURS

BEET TACOS

6 beets

2 tablespoons extra-virgin olive oil

2 tablespoons water

6 tablespoons fresh lime juice

1 tablespoon cumin

Salt and pepper, to taste

Tortillas, for serving

1   Preheat the oven to 400°F. Place the beets on a large piece of aluminum foil and form the foil into a pouch. Add the olive oil and water, seal the pouch, and place it in a baking pan.

2   Place the beets in the oven and roast until a knife inserted into them passes easily to their centers, 45 minutes to 1 hour.

3   Remove the beets from the oven and let them cool.

4   When the beets are cool enough to handle, peel them and cut them into bite-size pieces. Place the beets in a shallow bowl, add the lime juice and cumin, and season with salt and pepper. Stir to combine and let the beets marinate for 3 to 5 hours.

5   Serve with tortillas and your favorite taco fixings.

YIELD:
4 SERVINGS

ACTIVE TIME:
15 MINUTES

TOTAL TIME:
1 HOUR

SWEET POTATO TACOS

1½ lbs. sweet potatoes, peeled and diced

¾ cup pineapple juice

¼ cup dark brown sugar

1 teaspoon pure vanilla extract

4 tablespoons unsalted butter, diced

Tortillas, for serving

1   Preheat the oven to 375°F. Place the sweet potatoes in a large saucepan and cover them with cold water. Bring to a boil, reduce the heat so that the water simmers, and cook until the sweet potatoes are al dente, 6 to 8 minutes.

2   Drain the sweet potatoes and place them in a baking dish. Add the pineapple juice, brown sugar, vanilla, and butter and stir to combine. Place the dish in the oven and bake the sweet potatoes until they are glazed and fork-tender, 30 to 35 minutes, stirring occasionally.

3   Remove the sweet potatoes from the oven and serve with tortillas and your favorite taco fixings.

SWEET POTATO TACOS, SEE PAGE 53

YIELD:
8 SERVINGS

ACTIVE TIME:
30 MINUTES

TOTAL TIME:
28 HOURS

COCHINITA PIBIL TACOS

6 lbs. pork shoulder, cubed

Salt, to taste

Recado Rojo (see page 239)

1 package of banana leaves

1 large white onion, julienned

Tortillas, for serving

1   Place the pork shoulder in a large mixing bowl and season it generously with salt. Pour the Recado Rojo over the pork and rub it into the meat. Place the pork in the refrigerator and let it marinate for 24 hours.

2   Preheat the oven to 300°F. Remove the spines from the banana leaves and gently toast them over an open flame until they are pliable and bright green. Line a Dutch oven with the banana leaves, place the pork on top, and cover the pork with the onion. Fold the banana leaves over the pork to create a packet. Cover the Dutch oven, place it in the oven, and roast until the pork is fork-tender, 2 to 3 hours.

3   Remove the lid from the Dutch oven and open the banana leaf packet. Raise the oven's temperature to 400°F and roast the pork until the top is crispy, about 20 minutes.

4   Remove the pork from the oven and shred it with two forks. Serve with tortillas and your favorite taco fixings.

YIELD:
4 SERVINGS

ACTIVE TIME:
30 MINUTES

TOTAL TIME:
2 HOURS

CHILIBUL TACOS

2 lbs. skirt steak

1 white onion, quartered

1 head of garlic, halved

2 bay leaves

1 teaspoon dried marjoram

1 teaspoon dried oregano

1 teaspoon dried thyme

2 dried chipotle chile peppers, stems and seeds removed

Salt, to taste

1 lb. cooked or canned black beans, mashed

½ lb. chipotles en adobo, pureed

Tortillas, for serving

1   Place the steak in a large saucepan with the onion, garlic, bay leaves, marjoram, oregano, thyme, and dried chiles. Season with salt, cover the steak with water by 2 inches, and bring to a gentle simmer.

2   Cover the pan and simmer until the steak is tender and easy to shred with a fork, 1 to 2 hours. Let the steak cool in the liquid.

3   Remove the steak from the cooking liquid and shred it.

4   Place the steak, beans, and pureed chipotles in a saucepan, bring to a gentle simmer, and cook until everything is warmed through, 15 to 20 minutes.

5   Season the chilibul with salt and serve with tortillas and your favorite taco fixings.

CHILIBUL TACOS, SEE PAGE 57

YIELD:
4 SERVINGS

ACTIVE TIME:
30 MINUTES

TOTAL TIME:
4 HOURS

CECINA DE CERDO TACOS

7 oz. guajillo chile peppers, stems and seeds removed

1 teaspoon cumin seeds

1 teaspoon coriander seeds

1 bay leaves

2 tablespoons extra-virgin olive oil, plus more as needed

4 garlic cloves, minced

10 dried chiles de árbol, stems and seeds removed

7 tablespoons apple cider or champagne vinegar

Salt, to taste

2 lbs. pork tenderloin, pounded until ¼-inch thick, sliced

Tortillas, for serving

1   Place the guajillo chiles in a dry skillet and toast them over medium heat until they darken and become fragrant and pliable. Place the chiles in a bowl of hot water and let them soak for 30 minutes.

2   Place the cumin and coriander seeds and bay leaf in the dry skillet and toast until fragrant, shaking the pan frequently. Grind them into a powder using a mortar and pestle or a spice grinder.

3   Place the olive oil in a Dutch oven and warm it over medium heat. Add the garlic and cook, stirring continually, for 1 minute. Add the chiles de arbol and cook for 30 seconds. Remove the pan from heat.

4   Drain the guajillo chiles and reserve the soaking liquid. Place the guajillo, chiles de árbol, spice powder, and garlic in a blender and puree until the mixture is smooth and thick, adding the vinegar and soaking liquid as needed to attain the right consistency. Season the puree with salt.

5   Place the pork in a baking dish and pour the puree over it. Stir until it is coated and let it marinate in the refrigerator for 2 hours.

6   Preheat a charcoal or gas grill to medium-high heat (about 450°F). Lightly brush the grates with olive oil, place the pork on the grill, and grill until its interior is 145°F, 4 to 8 minutes per side.

7   Remove the pork from the grill and let it rest for 5 minutes. Serve with tortillas and your favorite taco fixings.

YIELD:
8 SERVINGS

ACTIVE TIME:
30 MINUTES

TOTAL TIME:
2 HOURS AND 30 MINUTES

PIERNA DE PUERCO TACOS

2 ancho chile peppers, stems and seeds removed

1 cascabel chile pepper, stem and seeds removed

1 chipotle mortia chile pepper, stem and seeds removed

1 guajillo chile pepper, stem and seeds removed

½ teaspoon black peppercorns

1½ teaspoons coriander seeds

1 teaspoon cumin seeds

½ teaspoon cinnamon

½ teaspoon ground cloves

8 garlic cloves

½ cup white vinegar

1 cup mezcal

Salt, to taste

8 lbs. pork shoulder, cubed

½ white onion, chopped

4 bay leaves

1 tablespoon all-purpose flour

1   Place the chiles in a bowl of hot water and let them soak for 20 minutes.

2   Place the black peppercorns, coriander, and cumin in a dry skillet and toast until fragrant, shaking the pan frequently.

3   Drain the chiles and place them in a blender along with the toasted spices, cinnamon, cloves, garlic, vinegar, and mezcal. Puree until smooth and season the puree generously with salt.

4   Place the pork shoulder in a large baking dish, rub the puree over it, and let it marinate for 1 hour.

5   Place the pork shoulder and marinade in a large pot, add water until the pork is completely covered, and then add the onion and bay leaves. Bring the water to a boil, reduce the heat so that it simmers, and cook the pork until it is fork-tender, about 1 hour.

6   Stir in the flour and cook until the sauce has thickened slightly. Taste, adjust the seasoning as needed, and shred with pork with two forks. Stir the pork back into the sauce and serve with tortillas and your favorite taco fixings.

YIELD:
8 SERVINGS

ACTIVE TIME:
15 MINUTES

TOTAL TIME:
1 HOUR

CARNE EN SU JUGO TACOS

3 tomatillos, husked and rinsed well

4 garlic cloves

2 serrano chile peppers, stems and seeds removed, minced

Salt, to taste

¼ cup extra-virgin olive oil

1 lb. bacon, chopped

4 lbs. beef chuck, cut into 2-inch-long strips

1 onion, finely diced

1 bunch of fresh cilantro, chopped

1 lb. cooked or canned pinto beans

Tortillas, for serving

1   Place the tomatillos, garlic, and chiles in a medium saucepan with enough water to cover everything, bring to a boil, and cook until the tomatillos are tender, about 10 minutes. Drain, transfer the vegetables to a blender, and puree until smooth. Season the puree with salt and set it aside.

2   Place the olive oil in a Dutch oven and warm it over medium-low heat. Add the bacon and cook, stirring occasionally, until it is golden brown, about 10 minutes. Remove the bacon from the pot and set it aside.

3   Drain any excess fat from the pot, raise the heat to high, and add the beef. Sear until it is browned all over, turning it as necessary. Remove the beef from the pot and set it aside.

4   Add the onion to the Dutch oven and cook until it starts to soften, about 5 minutes. Return the beef and bacon to the pot, pour the puree over everything, and, if necessary, add water until the beef is completely covered.

5   Cook over low heat until the beef is very tender, about 40 minutes.

6   Stir in the cilantro and pinto beans and cook until the beans are warmed through. Taste, adjust the seasoning as necessary, and serve with tortillas and your favorite taco fixings.

YIELD:
6 SERVINGS

ACTIVE TIME:
15 MINUTES

TOTAL TIME:
2 HOURS AND 15 MINUTES

CHILORIO TACOS

4 lbs. boneless pork shoulder, cut into 4 pieces

Salt, to taste

2 tablespoons extra-virgin olive oil

4 guajillo chile peppers, stems and seeds removed

2 ancho chile peppers, stems and seeds removed

6 garlic cloves

¼ white onion

2 cups orange juice

¼ cup white vinegar

1 tablespoon dried oregano

1½ teaspoons cumin

1½ teaspoons black pepper

Tortillas, for serving (optional)

1   Season the pork with salt and let it sit at room temperature.

2   Place the olive oil in a Dutch oven and warm it over medium heat. Add the chiles and fry until they are fragrant, stirring occasionally.

3   Transfer the chiles to a blender, add the remaining ingredients, except for the tortillas, and puree until smooth.

4   Working with one piece of pork at a time, place it in the Dutch oven and sear until it is browned on all sides.

5   Pour the puree over the pork. If the pork is not covered, add water until it is.

6   Cover the Dutch oven and cook the pork over low heat until it is tender and falling apart, about 2 hours.

7   Shred the pork with 2 forks and serve with tortillas and your favorite taco fixings.

CHILORIO TACOS, SEE PAGE 65

YIELD:
6 SERVINGS

ACTIVE TIME:
30 MINUTES

TOTAL TIME:
3 TO 4 HOURS

OCTOPUS AL PASTOR TACOS

1   Place the allspice, cloves, and cinnamon stick in a dry skillet and toast until they are fragrant, shaking the pan frequently. Grind the toasted spices into a powder using a mortar and pestle or a spice grinder.

2   Place the chiles in the dry skillet and toast over medium heat until they darken and become fragrant and pliable. Transfer them to a bowl of hot water and let them soak for 30 minutes.

3   Drain the chiles and reserve the liquid. Add the chiles, toasted spice powder, juices, Recado Rojo, garlic cloves, and oregano to a blender and puree until smooth. Season the al pastor marinade with salt and set it aside.

4   Bring water to a boil in a large pot. Place the octopus in the boiling water and poach for 3 minutes. Remove the octopus and let it cool.

5   Preheat the oven to 300°F. Place the octopus, cilantro, bay leaves, head of garlic, and onion in a Dutch oven and add stock until half of the octopus is covered. Cover the Dutch oven, place it in the oven, and braise for 2 to 3 hours, until the thickest part of the tentacles is very tender. Remove the octopus from the braising liquid and let it cool.

6   Place the octopus in the al pastor marinade and let it marinate for 30 minutes.

7   Prepare a gas or charcoal grill for high heat (about 500°F). Remove the octopus from the marinade and shake to remove any excess. Place the octopus on the grill and grill until it is caramelized and crispy on all sides, 5 to 7 minutes, taking care not to let the octopus burn.

8   Serve with tortillas and your favorite taco fixings.

3 allspice berries

2 whole cloves

½ cinnamon stick

3 chipotle morita chile peppers

2 chiles de árbol

7 guajillo chile peppers

2 tablespoons fresh lime juice

2 tablespoons orange juice

2 tablespoons grapefruit juice

7 tablespoons pineapple juice

½ cup Recado Rojo (see page 239)

5 garlic cloves

⅛ teaspoon dried oregano

Salt, to taste

6 lb. octopus, beak removed and head cleaned

1 small bunch of fresh cilantro

3 bay leaves

1 head of garlic, halved and gently charred

1 white onion, quartered and charred

8 cups Chicken Stock (see page 240)

Tortillas, for serving

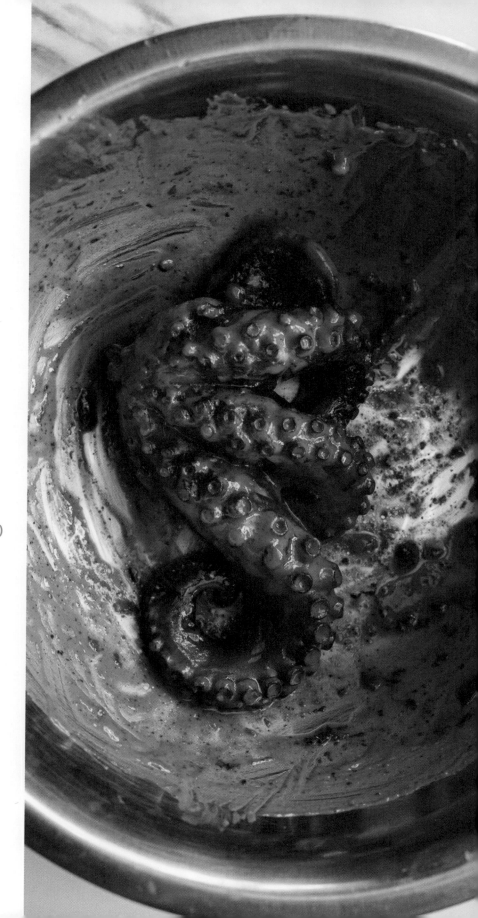

YIELD:
4 SERVINGS

ACTIVE TIME:
10 MINUTES

TOTAL TIME:
20 MINUTES

. . . .

BANG BANG SHRIMP TACOS

. . . .

½ cup all-purpose flour

Salt and pepper, to taste

½ cup cornstarch

Pinch of baking soda

1 teaspoon soy sauce

1 egg white

Canola oil, as needed

1 lb. large shrimp, shells removed, deveined

¼ cup sweet chili sauce

1 tablespoon rice vinegar

1 tablespoon sriracha

4 scallions, trimmed and sliced

2 large carrots, peeled and sliced thin

2 dried red chile peppers, stems and seeds removed, chopped

Tortillas, for serving

1   Place the flour in a shallow bowl, season it with salt and pepper, and stir to combine. Set the mixture aside.

2   Place the cornstarch and baking soda in another shallow bowl, season the mixture with salt and pepper, and stir to combine. While whisking continually, add the soy sauce and egg white until the mixture comes together as a smooth batter, adding water as needed to get the desired consistency.

3   Add canola oil to a Dutch oven until it is about 2 inches deep and warm it to 350°F.

4   Dredge the shrimp in the seasoned flour and then in the batter until they are evenly coated. Working in batches to avoid crowding the pot, gently slip the shrimp into the hot oil and fry until they are golden brown and cooked through, about 5 minutes.

5   Transfer the fried shrimp to a paper towel–lined plate and let them drain.

6   Place the chili sauce, vinegar, sriracha, and a splash of water in a small saucepan and warm the mixture over low heat. Stir in the scallions, carrots, and dried chiles and bring the sauce to a simmer. Cover the pan and cook until the vegetables are just tender, about 5 minutes.

7   Place the shrimp in a bowl, pour the sauce over them, and toss to coat. Serve with tortillas and your favorite taco fixings.

YIELD:
4 SERVINGS

ACTIVE TIME:
30 MINUTES

TOTAL TIME:
25 HOURS

RED SNAPPER TACOS

1 whole red snapper, scales removed, cleaned

1½ cups Recado Rojo (see page 239)

Banana leaves, as needed

2 habanero chile peppers, stemmed, seeded, and sliced

1 bunch of fresh cilantro

Salt, to taste

Tortillas, for serving

1   Rub the inside and outside of the snapper with the Recado Rojo. Let the fish marinate for 24 hours in the refrigerator.

2   Remove any stiff spines from the banana leaves and cut the leaves into pieces large enough to completely wrap up the fish. Toast the banana leaves over an open flame until they are bright green and very pliable.

3   Preheat the oven to 450°F. Place the fish in the banana leaves and top with the sliced habanero and cilantro. Season with salt, fold the banana leaves over so that they completely cover the fish, and tie the packet closed with kitchen twine.

4   Place the packet on a baking sheet, place it in the oven, and roast until the fish is just cooked through, 15 to 20 minutes, depending on the thickness of the fish. Remove the fish from the oven and let it rest in the packet for 5 minutes.

5   Open the packet, chop the snapper, and serve with tortillas and your favorite taco fixings.

RED SNAPPER TACOS, SEE PAGE 71

YIELD:
4 SERVINGS

ACTIVE TIME:
1 HOUR

TOTAL TIME:
8 HOURS

MUSHROOM BARBACOA TACOS

1 tablespoon coriander seeds

½ teaspoon whole cloves

½ teaspoon allspice berries

½ teaspoon cumin seeds

1½ tablespoons black peppercorns

1 ancho chile pepper, stem and seeds removed

1 guajillo chile pepper, stem and seeds removed

1 chipotle chile pepper, stem and seeds removed

1 pasilla chile pepper, stem and seeds removed

2 small onions, sliced

5 garlic cloves

1 cup orange juice

1 cup fresh lime juice

Salt, to taste

2¼ lbs. portobello mushrooms, sliced

Banana leaves, spines removed and toasted, as needed

2 bay leaves

Tortillas, for serving

1   Place the coriander, cloves, allspice, cumin, and peppercorns in a dry skillet and toast until they are fragrant, shaking the pan frequently. Use a mortar and pestle or a spice grinder to grind the mixture into a powder.

2   Place the chiles in the dry skillet and toast until they are fragrant and pliable. Transfer the chiles to a bowl of hot water and soak them for 20 minutes.

3   Drain the chiles and reserve the soaking liquid. Place the chiles, 1 onion, 2 garlic cloves, and some of the soaking liquid in a blender and puree until smooth. Add the toasted spice powder, and orange and lime juices, and pulse until incorporated.

4   Season the mixture with salt and place it in a mixing bowl. Add the mushrooms and let them marinate for 6 hours.

5   Preheat the oven to 420°F. Remove the mushrooms from the marinade and place them in the banana leaves. Layer the remaining onion and garlic and the bay leaves on top, fold the banana leaves over the mushrooms to form a packet, and tie it closed with kitchen twine.

6   Place the packet on a parchment-lined baking sheet, place it in the oven, and roast for 20 minutes.

7   Remove the packet from the oven and open it up. Return it to the oven and roast for an additional 10 to 15 minutes to caramelize the mushrooms.

8   Remove the mushrooms from the oven and serve with tortillas and your favorite taco fixings.

YIELD:
6 SERVINGS

ACTIVE TIME:
30 MINUTES

TOTAL TIME:
24 HOURS

BEEF BARBACOA TACOS

5 lbs. beef chuck, trimmed and cubed

Salt and pepper, to taste

1 teaspoon grated fresh ginger

2 whole cloves

1 teaspoon allspice

¼ cup red wine vinegar

2 garlic cloves

½ (4 oz.) bag of pickling spices

4 dried New Mexico chile peppers, stems and seeds removed

1 teaspoon sesame seeds

¾ cup water

¼ cup all-purpose flour

⅓ cup chili powder

6 bay leaves

Tortillas, for serving

1   Place the beef in a large mixing bowl and season it with salt and pepper.

2   Place the ginger, cloves, allspice, vinegar, garlic, pickling spices, chiles, sesame seeds, water, flour, and chili powder in a blender and puree until smooth.

3   Pour the puree over the beef and stir until it is coated. Cover the bowl with plastic wrap and let it marinate in the refrigerator overnight.

4   Preheat the oven to 350°F. Place the beef in a large roasting pan and add the bay leaves and about 6 cups water. Cover the pan with aluminum foil, place in the oven, and braise until the beef is falling apart, about 4 hours.

5   Remove the pan from the oven, use 2 forks to shred the beef, and serve with tortillas and your favorite taco fixings.

YIELD:
4 SERVINGS

ACTIVE TIME:
25 MINUTES

TOTAL TIME:
1 HOUR AND 30 MINUTES

POPCORN CHICKEN TACOS

3 garlic cloves, smashed

1 egg white

1 tablespoon soy sauce

1½ tablespoons sesame oil

½ teaspoon white pepper

1 tablespoon cornstarch

Salt, to taste

1 lb. boneless, skin-on chicken breasts, cut into bite-sized pieces

7 tablespoons tapioca starch, plus more as needed

Canola oil, as needed

Tortillas, for serving

1   Place the garlic, egg white, soy sauce, sesame oil, white pepper, cornstarch, and salt in a mixing bowl and stir to combine. Add the chicken, toss to coat, and cover the bowl. Place the bowl in the refrigerator and let the chicken marinate for 1 hour.

2   Dust a baking sheet with the tapioca starch, add the chicken, and dredge it in the tapioca starch until it is evenly coated. Add more tapioca starch as necessary.

3   Add canola oil to a Dutch oven until it is about 2 inches deep and warm it to 350°F. Shake the chicken to remove any excess tapioca starch, gently slip it into the hot oil, and fry until it is golden brown and cooked through, 8 to 10 minutes.

4   Place the fried chicken on a paper towel–lined plate to drain and briefly let it cool before serving with tortillas and your favorite taco fixings.

YIELD:
4 SERVINGS

ACTIVE TIME:
30 MINUTES

TOTAL TIME:
1 HOUR AND 30 MINUTES

SPICY SHRIMP TACOS

4 guajillo chile peppers, stems and seeds removed

6 garlic cloves

2 small Roma tomatoes

3 tablespoons chopped chipotles in adobo

Salt, to taste

1 lb. large shrimp, shells removed, deveined

¼ cup lard

Tortillas, for serving

1   Place the guajillo chiles in a dry skillet and toast them over medium heat until they darken and become fragrant and pliable.

2   Remove the chiles from the pan, place them in a bowl of hot water, and let them soak for 15 to 20 minutes.

3   Drain the chiles and reserve the soaking liquid. Add the guajillo chiles to a blender along with the garlic, tomatoes, chipotles, and a small amount of the soaking liquid and puree until the mixture is a smooth paste. Season the marinade with salt and let it cool completely.

4   Place the shrimp in the adobo and let them marinate for 30 minutes.

5   Place some of the lard in a large skillet and warm it over medium-high heat. Working in batches to avoid crowding the pan, add the shrimp and cook until they are just firm and turn pink, 3 to 5 minutes. Add more lard to the pan if it starts to look dry.

6   Serve with tortillas and your favorite taco fixings.

YIELD:
4 SERVINGS

ACTIVE TIME:
45 MINUTES

TOTAL TIME:
3 HOURS

LOBSTER & STREET CORN TACOS

FOR THE CORN

¼ cup mayonnaise

¼ cup crema or sour cream

1 teaspoon fresh lime juice

¼ teaspoon hot sauce

½ cup grated queso enchilado

Salt and pepper, to taste

Kernels from 2 ears of corn

2 tablespoons unsalted butter, melted

FOR THE LOBSTER

½ cup unsalted butter

6 oz. lobster tail

Tortillas, for serving

1   Preheat the oven to 375°F. To begin preparations for the corn, place the mayonnaise, crema, lime juice, hot sauce, queso enchilado, salt, and pepper in a salad bowl, stir to combine, and set the mixture aside.

2   Place the corn in small mixing bowl along with the butter and toss to combine. Place the corn in an even layer on a baking sheet, place it in the oven, and roast until it is golden brown, 25 to 30 minutes.

3   Remove the corn from the oven and transfer it to the salad bowl. Let the mixture cool and then chill it in the refrigerator for 2 hours.

4   To begin preparations for the lobster, place the butter in a skillet and melt it over medium-low heat.

5   Remove the meat from the lobster tail using kitchen scissors. Add the lobster meat to the pan and poach until it turns a reddish orange, 4 to 5 minutes. Remove the lobster meat from the pan with a slotted spoon and let it cool.

6   Slice the lobster into small medallions. Remove the corn mixture from the refrigerator, stir the lobster into it, and serve with tortillas and your favorite taco fixings.

YIELD:
4 SERVINGS

ACTIVE TIME:
15 MINUTES

TOTAL TIME:
4 HOURS AND 15 MINUTES

CHIPOTLE CHICKEN TACOS

1½ lbs. boneless, skinless chicken thighs

3 tablespoons honey

1 teaspoon onion powder

1 teaspoon garlic powder

½ teaspoon cumin

Salt, to taste

2 chipotles in adobo, chopped

2 tablespoons adobo

Tortillas, for serving

1   Place all of the ingredients, except for the tortillas, in a slow cooker and stir to combine. Cook on low until the chicken is extremely tender, about 4 hours.

2   Remove the chicken from the slow cooker, shred it with forks, and serve with tortillas and your favorite taco fixings.

YIELD:
4 SERVINGS

ACTIVE TIME:
15 MINUTES

TOTAL TIME:
25 MINUTES

TOFU TACOS

2 tablespoons avocado oil

1 lb. extra-firm tofu, crumbled

1 large onion, chopped

Salt and pepper, to taste

3 tablespoons tomato paste

2 teaspoons cumin

2 teaspoons ancho chile powder

1 teaspoon smoked paprika

1 teaspoon hot sauce

Tortillas, for serving

1 Place the avocado oil in a large skillet and warm it over medium-high heat. Add the tofu and onion, season with salt and pepper, and cook, without stirring, until the tofu starts to brown, about 2 minutes. Stir and cook until the tofu is browned all over, 3 to 5 minutes.

2 Stir in the tomato paste, cumin, chili powder, paprika, and hot sauce and cook, stirring continually, until the tofu is a deep red and beginning to stick to the skillet, 5 to 7 minutes.

3 Serve with tortillas and your favorite taco fixings.

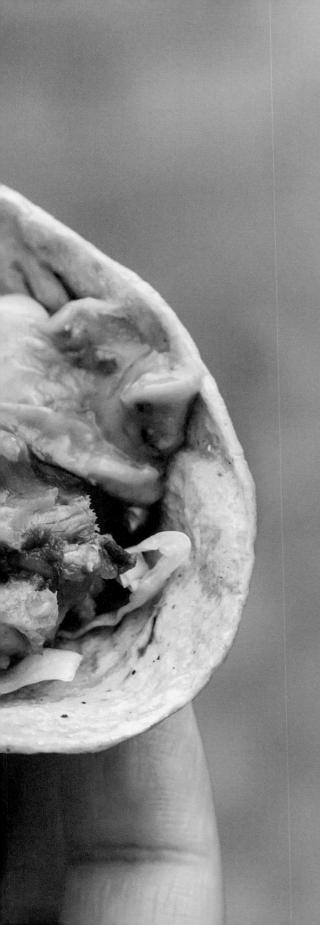

TOFU TACOS, SEE PAGE 85

YIELD:
4 SERVINGS

ACTIVE TIME:
15 MINUTES

TOTAL TIME:
30 MINUTES

TUNA TACOS

1 lb. tuna loin, sliced

Salt, to taste

3 tablespoons guajillo chile powder

¼ cup fresh lime juice

¼ cup orange juice

1 bay leaf

¼ cup lard

Tortillas, for serving

1   Season the tuna with salt and the guajillo powder. Combine the juices in a mixing bowl, add the tuna and bay leaf, and let the tuna marinate for 15 minutes.

2   Place the lard in a skillet and warm it over high heat. Add the tuna and sear it until the exterior is crispy and caramelized and the interior is rare, 2 to 3 minutes, turning it as necessary.

3   Serve with tortillas and your favorite taco fixings.

YIELD:
4 SERVINGS

ACTIVE TIME:
15 MINUTES

TOTAL TIME:
2 HOURS AND 45 MINUTES

CHICKEN TIKKA MASALA TACOS

2 lbs. boneless, skinless chicken thighs, chopped

3 tablespoons yogurt

3 tablespoons garam masala

¼ cup avocado oil

1 onion, diced

2 red chile peppers, stems and seeds removed, diced

1 tablespoon grated fresh ginger

3 garlic cloves, grated

2 teaspoons kosher salt

1 tablespoon brown sugar

2 teaspoons turmeric

1 tablespoon Kashmiri chili powder

2 tablespoons tomato paste

2 (14 oz.) cans of diced tomatoes

10 curry leaves

½ cup fresh cilantro

Tortillas, for serving

1   Place the chicken, yogurt, and 2 tablespoons of garam masala in a large mixing bowl and stir until well combined. Cover the bowl and let the chicken marinate in the refrigerator for 2 hours.

2   Place half of the avocado oil in a large skillet and warm it over medium-high heat. Add the onion and cook, stirring occasionally, until it is translucent, about 2 minutes. Add the remaining garam masala, the chiles, ginger, garlic, and salt and cook, stirring continually, for 2 minutes.

3   Add the brown sugar, turmeric, and chili powder and cook, stirring continually, for 2 minutes. Stir in the tomato paste and tomatoes and cook, stirring occasionally, for 4 minutes.

4   Pour the mixture into a blender and puree until it is very smooth, about 2 minutes.

5   Place the remaining avocado oil in a large skillet and warm it over medium heat. Add the chicken and cook until it is browned all over, turning it as necessary.

6   Add the puree, curry leaves, and cilantro. Simmer until the chicken is cooked through, about 20 minutes.

7   Serve with tortillas and your favorite taco fixings.

A taco is a tortilla and a delicious filling, sure. But it is really a blank canvas, an opportunity for everyone to indulge every single whim, and tailor a dish precisely to their taste.

The preparations in this chapter are what allow that tailoring to take place. Featuring salsas that run from fresh and spicy to bright and sweet, condiments that can supply either a luscious, creamy quality or a pleasant crunch, and the ultimate taco topping—Pickled Red Onion—everything you need to construct the ideal taco can be found in the following pages.

YIELD:
4 SERVINGS

ACTIVE TIME:
20 MINUTES

TOTAL TIME:
30 MINUTES

CHULIBU'UL

2 tablespoons lard

3 cups corn kernels

1 green bell pepper, stem and seeds removed, finely diced

1 small white onion, finely diced

2 tomatoes, chopped

1 (14 oz.) can of black-eyed peas, drained and rinsed

2 teaspoons dried oregano

1 teaspoon kosher salt

½ teaspoon dried savory

¼ teaspoon black pepper

1　Place the lard in a large skillet and warm it over medium-high heat. Add the corn and cook, stirring occasionally, until it begins to brown, 3 to 5 minutes.

2　Add the bell pepper and onion and cook until they begin to soften, 3 to 5 minutes, stirring occasionally.

3　Add the tomatoes and cook until they collapse, about 7 minutes.

4　Stir in the black-eyed peas, oregano, salt, savory, and black pepper, cook until everything is warmed through, and serve immediately.

YIELD:
1 CUP

ACTIVE TIME:
10 MINUTES

TOTAL TIME:
25 MINUTES

PICO DE GALLO

1 cup cherry tomatoes, chopped

½ onion, finely diced

2 jalapeño chile peppers, stems and seeds removed, finely diced

Salt, to taste

1 cup fresh cilantro, chopped

1 Place the tomatoes, onion, and chiles in a small mixing bowl and stir to combine.

2 Season the pico de gallo with salt, stir in the cilantro, and refrigerate the salsa for 15 minutes before serving.

PICO DE GALLO, SEE PAGE 95

YIELD:
2 CUPS

ACTIVE TIME:
10 MINUTES

TOTAL TIME:
10 MINUTES

SALSA DE AGUACATE

½ lb. tomatillos, husked and rinsed

½ white onion

4 garlic cloves

⅔ cup diced avocado

4 cups fresh cilantro

Fresh lime juice, to taste

Salt, to taste

1 Place the tomatillos, onion, garlic, and avocado in a food processor and blitz until pureed.

2 Add the cilantro and pulse to incorporate. Season the salsa with lime juice and salt and either serve it immediately or store in the refrigerator.

YIELD:
4 SERVINGS

ACTIVE TIME:
40 MINUTES

TOTAL TIME:
2 DAYS

PICKLED PINEAPPLE

2 star anise pods

½ cinnamon stick

2 chiles de árbol

2¼ cups apple cider vinegar

7 tablespoons white vinegar

3 tablespoons sugar

Salt, to taste

1 pineapple, peeled, cored, and sliced

1   Prepare a gas or charcoal grill for medium heat (400°F).

2   Place the star anise, cinnamon stick, and chiles in a saucepan and toast until they are fragrant, shaking the pan frequently.

3   Add the vinegars and sugar, generously season with salt, and bring to a boil, stirring to dissolve the sugar. Pour the brine into a sterilized mason jar.

4   Place the pineapple on the grill and grill until it is charred on both sides, about 8 minutes, turning it over halfway through. Add the pineapple to the brine while it is still warm and let the mixture cool to room temperature. Cover the jar and refrigerate the pineapple for 2 days before serving.

YIELD:
4 SERVINGS

ACTIVE TIME:
15 MINUTES

TOTAL TIME:
4 HOURS AND 30 MINUTES

ESCABECHE

1 carrot, peeled and sliced thin

1 cup cauliflower florets

1 radish, trimmed and sliced thin

6 green beans, chopped

½ jalapeño chile pepper, sliced thin

2 garlic cloves, smashed

1½ teaspoons sugar

½ teaspoon fine sea salt

½ teaspoon peppercorns

½ cup white vinegar

1 cup water

1   Layer the vegetables in a mason jar.

2   Place the remaining ingredients in a saucepan and bring to a boil over medium-high heat, stirring to dissolve the sugar. Pour the brine over the vegetables and let the escabeche cool to room temperature.

3   Cover the jar and chill it in the refrigerator for at least 4 hours before serving.

YIELD:
1½ CUPS

ACTIVE TIME:
20 MINUTES

TOTAL TIME:
1 HOUR

SALSA DE CHILTOMATE

8½ oz. Roma tomatoes, halved

2 habanero chile peppers

1 small white onion, quartered

4 garlic cloves, unpeeled

2 tablespoons extra-virgin olive oil

Salt, to taste

Juice of 1 lime

1   Preheat the oven to 450°F. Line a baking sheet with parchment paper, place the tomatoes, chiles, onion, and garlic on it, and place it in the oven.

2   Roast until the vegetables are charred all over, checking every 5 minutes or so and removing them as they become ready.

3   Peel the garlic cloves, remove the stem and seeds from the habanero, and place the roasted vegetables in a blender. Puree until smooth.

4   Place the olive oil in a medium saucepan and warm it over medium-high heat. Carefully pour the puree into the pan, reduce the heat, and simmer until the salsa reduces slightly and the flavor is to your liking, 15 to 20 minutes.

5   Season with salt, stir in the lime juice, and let the salsa cool. Taste, adjust the seasoning as necessary, and serve.

YIELD:
2 CUPS

ACTIVE TIME:
20 MINUTES

TOTAL TIME:
40 MINUTES

MOLE VERDE

¼ teaspoon whole cloves

¼ teaspoon allspice berries

¼ teaspoon cumin seeds

½ teaspoon coriander seeds

⅓ cup sesame seeds

3 tablespoons pepitas

Salt, to taste

1½ cups fresh epazote

½ cup fresh mint

½ cup fresh parsley

1 cup fresh hoja santa

2 cups fresh cilantro

2 oz. kale, stems and ribs removed

½ lb. tomatillos, husked and rinsed well

3 serrano chile peppers

10 garlic cloves

1 small white onion, quartered

1   Preheat the oven to 325°F. Place the cloves, allspice, cumin, and coriander in a dry skillet and toast until they are fragrant, shaking the pan frequently. Use a mortar and pestle or a spice grinder to grind the mixture into a fine powder.

2   Place the sesame seeds and pepitas on a parchment-lined baking sheet, place it in the oven, and toast until just golden brown, about 7 minutes. Remove from the oven and let the seeds cool.

3   Prepare an ice bath and bring generously salted water to a simmer in a large saucepan. Add the fresh herbs and kale and blanch for 30 to 45 seconds. Drain the mixture and shock it in the ice bath. Place the mixture in a linen towel and wring the towel to extract as much water from the mixture as possible. Transfer it to a blender.

4   Place the tomatillos, chiles, garlic, and onion in a saucepan and cover by 1 inch with water. Season the water with salt and bring to a simmer. Cook until the vegetables are tender, about 15 minutes. Drain and add them to the blender.

5   Add the toasted seeds and fine spice powder to the blender and puree until smooth. Season the mole with salt and gently warm it before serving.

YIELD:
4 SERVINGS

ACTIVE TIME:
5 MINUTES

TOTAL TIME:
50 MINUTES

MARINATED RADISHES

2 watermelon radishes, trimmed and sliced thin

½ cup extra-virgin olive oil

¼ cup honey

2 teaspoons rice vinegar

2 teaspoons soy sauce

1 teaspoon sesame oil

1 teaspoon grated fresh ginger

2 teaspoons minced shallot

1   Place the radishes in a bowl. Place the olive oil, honey, vinegar, soy sauce, sesame oil, ginger, and shallot in a separate bowl and whisk to combine.

2   Pour the mixture over the radishes and let them marinate for 45 minutes before serving.

MARINATED RADISHES, SEE PAGE 107

YIELD:
4 CUPS

ACTIVE TIME:
30 MINUTES

TOTAL TIME:
2 TO 3 DAYS

PIKLIZ

¼ **head of cabbage, sliced thin**

1 large carrot, peeled and shredded

2 large shallots, sliced

¼ **red bell pepper, sliced**

¼ **green bell pepper, sliced**

¼ **orange bell pepper, sliced**

2 scotch bonnet or habanero chile peppers, stems and seeds removed, sliced

Juice of 1 lime

4 cups white vinegar

2 teaspoons kosher salt

1 Place the cabbage, carrot, shallots, and bell peppers in a large bowl.

2 Place the chile peppers, lime juice, and ¼ cup of the vinegar in a microwave-safe bowl. Place the bowl in the microwave and microwave for 2 minutes, which will bring out all of the spice in the peppers. Remove the bowl from the microwave and let the mixture cool completely.

3 Pour the chile pepper mixture over the sliced vegetables and stir to combine. Add the remaining vinegar until the mixture is completely covered and then stir in the salt.

4 Cover the bowl with plastic wrap, place it in the refrigerator, and let the pikliz marinate for 48 to 72 hours before serving.

YIELD:
1 CUP

ACTIVE TIME:
5 MINUTES

TOTAL TIME:
5 MINUTES

CILANTRO CREMA

2 tablespoons chopped fresh cilantro

1 cup sour cream

½ teaspoon kosher salt

1 teaspoon sugar

2 teaspoons fresh lime juice

1 teaspoon lime zest

½ teaspoon smoked paprika

¼ teaspoon cayenne pepper

1   Place all of the ingredients in a food processor and blitz until combined. Serve immediately or store in the refrigerator.

YIELD:
2 CUPS

ACTIVE TIME:
10 MINUTES

TOTAL TIME:
40 MINUTES

SOS TI MALICE

1 teaspoon extra-virgin olive oil

1 small onion, sliced

2 scotch bonnet chile peppers or 2 habanero chile peppers, stems and seeds removed, sliced

½ small red bell pepper, sliced

3 garlic cloves, sliced

Salt and pepper, to taste

2 tablespoons tomato paste

2 tablespoons apple cider vinegar

1 tablespoon fresh lime juice

1 cup water, plus more as needed

1   Place the olive oil in a medium saucepan and warm it over medium heat. Add the onion, chiles, bell pepper, and garlic, season with salt and pepper, and cook for about 5 minutes.

2   Add the remaining ingredients and bring to a boil. Reduce the heat so that the mixture simmers and cook for about 20 minutes.

3   Transfer the mixture to a blender and puree on high until it is smooth. Add water as desired to achieve the right consistency.

4   Taste the hot sauce, adjust the seasoning as necessary, and use immediately or store in the refrigerator.

YIELD:
4 CUPS

ACTIVE TIME:
30 MINUTES

TOTAL TIME:
1 HOUR AND 30 MINUTES

CHILE COLORADO

7 oz. guajillo chile peppers, stems and seeds removed

1¾ oz. ancho chile peppers, stems and seeds removed

⅓ oz. chiles de árbol, stems and seeds removed

1 tablespoon coriander seeds

1½ teaspoons allspice berries

1¼ tablespoons cumin seeds

1 tablespoon extra-virgin olive oil

1 white onion, sliced

10 garlic cloves

1 tablespoon dried marjoram

1 tablespoon dried oregano

1 tablespoon dried thyme

3 tablespoons lard

2 bay leaves

Chicken Stock (see page 240), as needed

Salt, to taste

1 Place the chiles in a dry skillet and toast until they are pliable and fragrant, about 30 seconds. Place them in a bowl, cover them with hot water, and soak the chiles for 30 minutes.

2 Place the coriander seeds, allspice berries, and cumin seeds in the dry skillet and toast until they are fragrant, shaking the pan frequently to keep them from burning. Grind the toasted seeds into a fine powder using a mortar and pestle or a spice grinder.

3 Place the olive oil in the skillet and warm it over medium heat. Add the onion, garlic, toasted spice powder, marjoram, oregano, and thyme and cook, stirring frequently, until the onion is translucent, about 3 minutes.

4 Drain the chiles and reserve the soaking liquid. Place the chiles and onion mixture in a food processor and blitz until smooth, adding the reserved liquid as necessary to get the desired consistency.

5 Place the lard in a Dutch oven and warm it over high heat. Carefully add the puree (it will splatter) and the bay leaves, reduce the heat to low, and simmer the sauce for 1 hour, adding stock as necessary to get the flavor and texture to your liking. Season the sauce with salt before using or storing.

YIELD:
3 CUPS

ACTIVE TIME:
15 MINUTES

TOTAL TIME:
30 MINUTES

SWEET CORN & PEPITA GUACAMOLE

1 ear of yellow corn, with husk on

1 oz. pumpkin seeds

1 oz. pomegranate seeds

Flesh of 3 avocados

½ red onion, chopped

½ cup fresh cilantro, chopped

1 teaspoon fresh lime juice

Salt and pepper, to taste

1 Prepare a gas or charcoal grill for medium-high heat (about 450°F). Place the corn on the grill and cook until it is charred all over and the kernels have softened enough that there is considerable give in them.

2 Remove the corn from the grill and let it cool. When cool enough to handle, husk the corn and cut off the kernels.

3 Combine the corn, pumpkin seeds, and pomegranate seeds in a small bowl. Place the avocados in a separate bowl and mash until just slightly chunky. Stir in the corn mixture, onion, cilantro, and lime juice, season with salt and pepper, and work the mixture until the guacamole is the desired texture. Serve immediately.

SWEET CORN & PEPITA GUACAMOLE, SEE PAGE 117

YIELD:
1½ CUPS

ACTIVE TIME:
20 MINUTES

TOTAL TIME:
30 MINUTES

SALSA VERDE TATEMADA

1 lb. tomatillos, husked and rinsed well

5 garlic cloves, unpeeled

1 small white onion, quartered

10 serrano chile peppers

2 bunches of fresh cilantro

Salt, to taste

1 Warm a cast-iron skillet over high heat. Place the tomatillos, garlic, onion, and chiles in the pan and cook until charred all over, turning them as necessary.

2 Remove the vegetables from the pan and let them cool slightly.

3 Peel the garlic cloves and remove the stems and seeds from the chiles. Place the charred vegetables in a blender, add the cilantro, and puree until smooth.

4 Season the salsa with salt and serve immediately.

YIELD:
1½ CUPS

ACTIVE TIME:
20 MINUTES

TOTAL TIME:
1 HOUR AND 30 MINUTES

SALPICON DE RABANO Y CHILE HABANERO

2 habanero chile peppers

4 radishes, trimmed and julienned

1 bay leaf

½ teaspoon dried oregano

½ cup fresh lime juice

½ cup orange juice

1 tablespoon extra-virgin olive oil

Salt, to taste

1   Roast the habaneros over an open flame, in the oven, or on the grill until they are charred all over. Let them cool briefly.

2   Remove the stems and seeds, and mince the remaining flesh.

3   Place the habaneros in a bowl, add the remaining ingredients, and stir to combine. Refrigerate the salsa for at least 1 hour before serving.

YIELD:
1 CUP

ACTIVE TIME:
10 MINUTES

TOTAL TIME:
20 MINUTES

X'NIPEK

4 Roma tomatoes, seeds removed, diced

2 habanero chile peppers, stems and seeds removed, minced

1½ small red onions, julienned

1¼ cups fresh cilantro, chopped

1¾ oz. fresh lime juice

10 tablespoons orange juice

1½ teaspoons dried oregano

Salt, to taste

1 Place all of the ingredients, except for the salt, in a bowl and stir until combined. Let the mixture macerate for 10 minutes.

2 Season the salsa with salt and either serve it immediately or store in the refrigerator.

YIELD:
1 CUP

ACTIVE TIME:
20 MINUTES

TOTAL TIME:
1 HOUR

CHILES TOREADOS

10 serrano chile peppers

1 small white onion, quartered

3 garlic cloves, unpeeled

½ cup soy sauce

½ cup fresh lime juice

2 tablespoons Maggi seasoning sauce

1   Warm a cast-iron skillet over high heat. Place the chiles in the pan and toast until they are very charred all over, turning them as necessary. Remove the chiles from the pan and let them cool.

2   Place the onion and garlic cloves in the dry skillet and toast until they are lightly charred, turning them as necessary. Remove them from the pan and let them cool.

3   Peel the garlic cloves, mince them, and place them in a bowl. Julienne the onion and place it in the bowl.

4   Remove all but one-quarter of the charred skin from the chiles. Remove the stems and seeds and finely chop the remaining flesh. Add it to the garlic mixture along with the remaining ingredients and stir until combined.

5   Let the salsa macerate for 30 minutes before serving.

YIELD:
½ CUP

ACTIVE TIME:
10 MINUTES

TOTAL TIME:
30 MINUTES

SALSA DE ÁRBOL

¼ cup lard

3½ oz. chiles de árbol, stems and seeds removed

1 oz. guajillo chile peppers, stems and seeds removed

10 garlic cloves

Salt, to taste

1   Place the lard in a cast-iron skillet and warm it over medium heat. Add the chiles and fry until they are fragrant and pliable, about 30 seconds. Place the chiles in a bowl, cover them with hot water, and let them soak for 20 minutes.

2   Place the garlic in the skillet and fry, stirring continually, until it is fragrant, about 1 minute. Place it in a blender.

3   Drain the chiles and reserve the soaking liquid. Add the chiles to the blender and blitz until the mixture is smooth, adding the reserved liquid as needed to get the desired texture.

4   Season the salsa with salt and either serve it immediately or store in the refrigerator.

YIELD:
1½ CUPS

ACTIVE TIME:
20 MINUTES

TOTAL TIME:
30 MINUTES

SALSA BORRACHA

½ lb. tomatillos, husked and rinsed well

¾ small white onion

5 garlic cloves, unpeeled

2 tablespoons lard

3 pasilla chile peppers, stems and seeds removed

2 chipotle morita chile peppers, stems and seeds removed

3½ oz. Mexican lager

1 teaspoon mezcal or tequila

1 teaspoon Maggi seasoning sauce

Salt, to taste

1 Warm a cast-iron skillet over medium-high heat. Add the tomatillos, onion, and garlic and toast until they are charred all over, turning them as needed. Remove the vegetables from the pan and let them cool. When cool enough to handle, peel the garlic cloves and place the mixture in a blender.

2 Place half of the lard in the skillet and warm it over medium heat. Add the chiles and fry until they are fragrant and pliable. Place the chiles in the blender.

3 Add the beer, mezcal, and Maggi to the blender and puree until smooth.

4 Place the remaining lard in a saucepan and warm it over medium heat. Add the puree and fry it for 5 minutes. Season the salsa with salt and let it cool completely before serving.

YIELD:
2 CUPS

ACTIVE TIME:
15 MINUTES

TOTAL TIME:
45 MINUTES

MORITA SALSA

3½ oz. chipotle morita chile peppers, stems and seeds removed

5 Roma tomatoes, halved

1 small white onion, quartered

5 garlic cloves

Salt, to taste

1 Place the chiles in a dry skillet and gently toast until they are fragrant and pliable, about 30 seconds. Place the chiles in a bowl, cover them with hot water, and let them soak for 30 minutes.

2 Drain the chiles, place them in a food processor, and add the tomatoes, onion, and garlic. Blitz until pureed, season the salsa with salt, and either serve it immediately or store in the refrigerator.

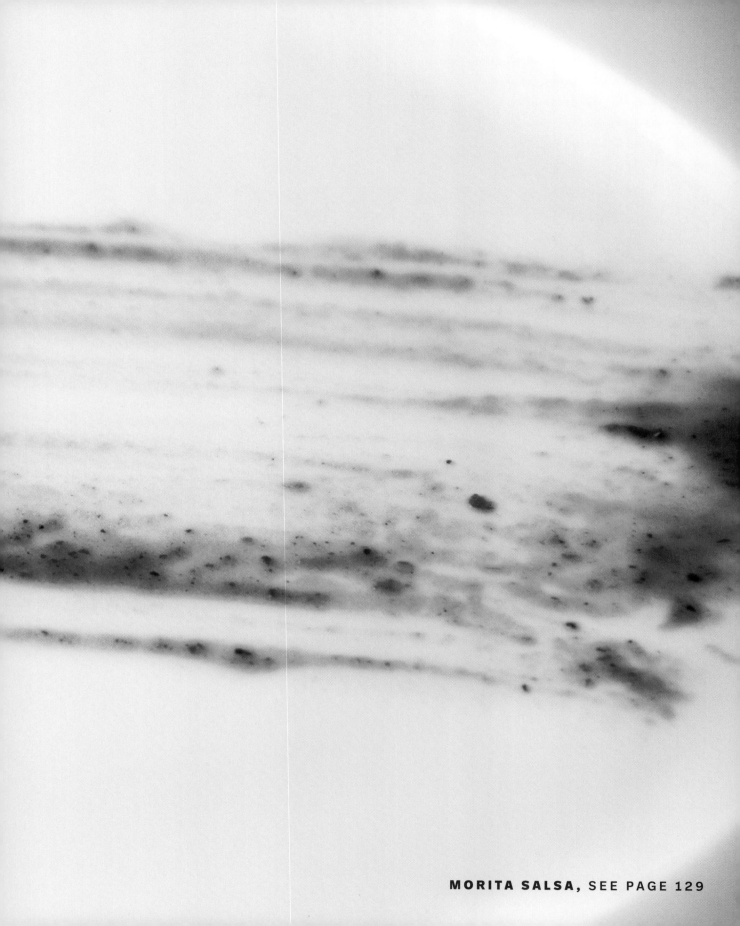

MORITA SALSA, SEE PAGE 129

YIELD:
2 CUPS

ACTIVE TIME:
10 MINUTES

TOTAL TIME:
3 TO 5 DAYS

FERMENTED CHILE ADOBO

13¼ cups water

⅓ cup kosher salt

2¼ lbs. chipotle morita chile peppers, stems and seeds removed

10 garlic cloves, smashed

1 cinnamon stick

¼ teaspoon whole cloves

2 bay leaves

½ cup apple cider vinegar

1 teaspoon dried oregano

1   Place the water and salt in a saucepan and bring it to a simmer, stirring to dissolve the salt. Turn off the heat and let the brine cool slightly.

2   Place the chiles and garlic in a fermentation crock or large container that has been sterilized. Cover the mixture with the brine and place some plastic wrap directly on the surface. Let the mixture sit at room temperature for 3 to 5 days.

3   Place the cinnamon stick, cloves, and bay leaves in a dry skillet and toast until they are fragrant, shaking the pan frequently. Use a mortar and pestle or spice grinder to grind the mixture into a fine powder.

4   Strain the liquid from the fermented mixture and reserve it.

5   Place the chiles and garlic in a food processor, add the toasted spice powder, vinegar, and oregano, and blitz until the mixture is smooth, adding the reserved liquid as needed to get the desired texture. Serve immediately or store in the refrigerator.

YIELD:
1½ CUPS

ACTIVE TIME:
30 MINUTES

TOTAL TIME:
30 MINUTES

DZIKIL P'AAK

3 Roma tomatoes

4 oz. tomatillos, husked and rinsed

¾ small white onion

4 garlic cloves, unpeeled

2 habanero chile peppers

7 oz. pepitas, roasted

7 tablespoons fresh lime juice

7 tablespoons orange juice

1½ cups fresh cilantro

1 teaspoon Maggi seasoning sauce

Salt, to taste

1   Warm a cast-iron skillet over medium-high heat. Add the tomatoes, tomatillos, onion, garlic, and habanero and toast until they are charred all over, turning them as needed.

2   Remove the vegetables from the pan and let them cool. When cool enough to handle, peel the garlic cloves, remove the stems and seeds from the habaneros, and place the mixture in a food processor.

3   Add the pumpkin seeds to the food processor and pulse until the mixture is a thick paste. Add the juices, cilantro, and Maggi sauce and pulse until the salsa has a hummus-like consistency.

4   Season the salsa with salt and either serve it immediately or store in the refrigerator.

DZIKIL P'AAK, SEE PAGE 133

YIELD:
2 CUPS

ACTIVE TIME:
10 MINUTES

TOTAL TIME:
2 HOURS

PICKLED RED ONION

½ cup apple cider vinegar

½ cup water

2 tablespoons kosher salt

2 tablespoons sugar

1 red onion, sliced thin

1   Place the vinegar, water, salt, and sugar in a saucepan and bring to a boil, stirring to dissolve the salt and sugar.

2   Place the onion in a mason jar, pour the brine over it, and let cool completely.

3   Let the onion cool completely before serving or storing in the refrigerator.

YIELD:
½ CUP

ACTIVE TIME:
15 MINUTES

TOTAL TIME:
25 MINUTES

SALSA MACHA

1 oz. white sesame seeds

¼ cup lard

¼ cup unsalted almonds

10 chiles de árbol, stems and seeds removed

1 ancho chile pepper, stem and seeds removed

2 garlic cloves, sliced thin

2 tablespoons white vinegar

1 teaspoon sugar

1   Place the sesame seeds in a dry skillet and toast them over low heat until they are toasted, shaking the pan as needed to keep them from burning. Remove the sesame seeds from the pan and set them aside.

2   Place the lard in the skillet and warm it over medium heat. Add the almonds and fry until they are golden brown, shaking the pan to prevent them from burning. Remove the almonds from the pan and set them aside.

3   Reduce the heat to low, add the chiles to the pan, and fry until they are fragrant and lightly toasted, about 30 seconds. Remove the chiles from the pan and set them aside.

4   Using a mortar and pestle, grind the sesame seeds, almonds, chiles, and the remaining ingredients together until the mixture is a slightly chunky puree. Serve the salsa immediately or store it in the refrigerator.

YIELD:
3 CUPS

ACTIVE TIME:
30 MINUTES

TOTAL TIME:
24 HOURS

QUESO FRESCO

8 cups whole milk

2 tablespoons kosher salt

1⅓ cups white vinegar

1   Place the milk and salt in a medium saucepan and bring to a gentle simmer over medium-low heat.

2   When the mixture reaches 180°F, remove the pan from heat, add the vinegar, and gently stir the mixture with a wooden spoon. You should see small curds begin to form. Cover the pan and let the mixture rest for 45 minutes.

3   Strain the curds into a fine sieve lined with cheesecloth. Let the curds release all of their liquid, using a small plate to weight down the curds.

4   Form the cheesecloth containing the curds into a bundle and let the cheese chill in the refrigerator overnight.

5   The cheese will be ready to crumble, shred, or break into chunks once fully cooled. Serve immediately or store in the refrigerator.

YIELD:
2 CUPS

ACTIVE TIME:
5 MINUTES

TOTAL TIME:
5 MINUTES

SALSA CRUDA VERDE

4 tomatillos, husked, rinsed well, and quartered

5 serrano chile peppers, stems and seeds removed

1 garlic clove

Flesh of ½ avocado

Salt, to taste

1   Place the tomatillos, serrano peppers, and garlic in a food processor and blitz until the mixture is combined but still chunky.

2   Add the avocado and pulse until incorporated.

3   Season the salsa with salt and either serve immediately or store it in the refrigerator.

YIELD:
2 CUPS

ACTIVE TIME:
5 MINUTES

TOTAL TIME:
2 HOURS

PICKLED MANZANO PEPPERS

4 manzano chile peppers, stems and seeds removed, sliced thin

½ cup apple cider vinegar

¼ cup water

1 tablespoon sugar

1 tablespoon kosher salt

1   Place the manzano peppers in a mason jar.

2   Place the remaining ingredients in a small saucepan and bring to a boil, stirring to dissolve the salt and sugar.

3   Pour the brine over the chiles, let them cool completely, and either serve immediately or store in the refrigerator.

YIELD:
2 CUPS

ACTIVE TIME:
20 MINUTES

TOTAL TIME:
2 HOURS

PICKLED RED CABBAGE

½ cup red wine vinegar

¼ cup canola oil

⅔ cup sugar

1½ teaspoons kosher salt

1½ teaspoons dry mustard

1 teaspoon celery seeds

½ teaspoon mustard seeds

½ cup Chicken Stock (see page 240)

¼ head of red cabbage, shredded

1 Place all of the ingredients, except for the cabbage, in a medium saucepan and bring to a boil.

2 Add the cabbage and cook until it is tender, about 20 minutes.

3 Pour the cabbage and brine into a mason jar and let it cool completely before serving or storing in the refrigerator.

PICKLED RED CABBAGE, SEE PAGE 145

YIELD:
2 CUPS

ACTIVE TIME:
15 MINUTES

TOTAL TIME:
15 MINUTES

GUACAMOLE

1 large tomato, finely diced

2 serrano chile peppers, stems and seeds removed, finely diced

½ onion, finely diced

1 garlic clove, mashed

Flesh of 4 large avocados

6 tablespoons fresh lime juice

Salt, to taste

½ cup fresh cilantro, chopped

1   Combine the tomato, chiles, and onion in a bowl. Place the garlic in a separate bowl.

2   Add the avocados to the bowl containing the garlic and stir until the mixture is well combined. Stir in the lime juice and season with salt.

3   Add the tomato mixture and stir until it has been incorporated. Add the cilantro and stir to combine.

4   Taste, adjust the seasoning as necessary, and serve immediately.

YIELD:
1 CUP

ACTIVE TIME:
10 MINUTES

TOTAL TIME:
2 HOURS

SPICY HONEY

4 chile peppers, minced

1 cup honey

1   Place the chiles and honey in a saucepan and bring to a very gentle simmer over medium-low heat. Reduce the heat to the lowest possible setting and cook for 1 hour.

2   Remove the saucepan from heat and let the mixture infuse for another hour.

3   Transfer the honey to a container, cover, and chill it in the refrigerator until it has completely cooled before serving.

YIELD:
2 CUPS

ACTIVE TIME:
25 MINUTES

TOTAL TIME:
2 WEEKS TO 1 MONTH

SPICY PRESERVED LIMES

7 limes

2 tablespoons ground cardamom seeds

2 tablespoons smoked paprika

2 tablespoons turmeric

1½ teaspoons cumin seeds, toasted and ground

3 tablespoons kosher salt

5 chiles de árbol, stems and seeds removed, ground

1   Juice the limes into a large bowl and save the spent halves. Add all of the remaining ingredients to the bowl and stir until the mixture is a paste.

2   Put on gloves, add the spent lime halves, and work the mixture with your hands until well combined.

3   Transfer the mixture to a sterilized airtight container and gently press down on it to make sure that the liquid is completely covering the solids and there are no pockets that air can get into.

4   Seal the container and store at room temperature or chill in the refrigerator until the lime halves are tender. This will take about 2 weeks at room temperature, and a month in the refrigerator.

5   Mince the limes and either serve immediately or store in the refrigerator.

YIELD:
2 CUPS

ACTIVE TIME:
5 MINUTES

TOTAL TIME:
35 MINUTES

MANGO SALSA

Flesh of 2 mangoes, diced

1 red chile pepper, stem and seeds removed, sliced thin

¼ cup chopped fresh cilantro, plus more for garnish

½ cup finely diced red onion

3½ tablespoons fresh lime juice

2 tablespoons fresh lemon juice

Salt and pepper, to taste

1   Place the mangoes, chile, cilantro, onion, lime juice, and lemon juice in a small bowl, season with salt and pepper, and gently toss to combine.

2   Cover the bowl with plastic wrap and chill the salsa in the refrigerator for 30 minutes before serving.

MANGO SALSA, SEE PAGE 153

YIELD:
2 CUPS

ACTIVE TIME:
5 MINUTES

TOTAL TIME:
5 MINUTES

PASILLA YOGURT

4 pasilla chile peppers, stems and seeds removed

2 cups yogurt

Juice of 1 lime

Salt, to taste

1   Place the chiles in a dry skillet and toast over medium heat until they are fragrant and pliable. Remove the chiles from the pan and let them cool.

2   Using a mortar and pestle, grind the chiles into a fine powder.

3   Add the pasilla powder to the yogurt and fold to combine. Stir in the lime juice and season the mixture with salt. Serve the yogurt immediately or store in the refrigerator.

YIELD:
1 CUP

ACTIVE TIME:
5 MINUTES

TOTAL TIME:
5 MINUTES

LIME CREMA

1 cup crema (Mexican sour cream)

3 tablespoons fresh lime juice

Salt, to taste

1   Place all of the ingredients in a small bowl, stir to combine, and either serve the crema immediately or store in the refrigerator.

LIME CREMA, SEE PAGE 157

YIELD:
4 CUPS

ACTIVE TIME:
30 MINUTES

TOTAL TIME:
2 HOURS

STRAWBERRY HOT SAUCE

1 lb. strawberries, rinsed and hulled

2 teaspoons kosher salt, plus more to taste

3½ oz. chiles de árbol

4 cups water

1½ teaspoons cumin

1 tablespoon coriander

1¼ cups plus 1 tablespoon apple cider vinegar

1¾ cups white vinegar

1   Place the strawberries and salt in a food processor and blitz until smooth. Let the mixture sit at room temperature for 1 hour.

2   Place the chiles, strawberry puree, and water in a saucepan and bring the mixture to a boil, making sure to stir and scrape the bottom of the pan frequently to keep a skin from forming.

3   Add the cumin and coriander and cook for another 20 minutes, stirring the sauce and scraping the bottom of the pan frequently.

4   Working in batches, transfer the sauce to the blender and puree for about 3 minutes. The strawberry seeds should break down, as they have been cooking for a while.

5   Strain the mixture through a fine-mesh sieve into a clean saucepan. Add the vinegars and cook over medium-high heat until the sauce has reduced by half.

6   Season the sauce generously with salt and serve immediately, or let it cool and store it in the refrigerator.

YIELD:
2 CUPS

ACTIVE TIME:
25 MINUTES

TOTAL TIME:
1 HOUR AND 30 MINUTES

GRILLED CORN & JALAPEÑO SALSA

2 ears of corn, shucked

1 tablespoon extra-virgin olive oil

Salt and pepper, to taste

1 small jalapeño chile pepper, stem and seeds removed, diced, plus more for garnish

¼ cup diced red onion

1 garlic clove, minced

1½ tablespoons fresh lime juice

¼ cup chopped fresh cilantro, plus more for garnish

½ cup diced tomato

1   Prepare a gas or charcoal grill for medium heat (about 400°F). Place the corn on the grill and cook until the ears are charred all over and just tender, about 15 minutes, turning them as necessary. Remove the corn from the grill and let them cool briefly.

2   Cut the kernels off the cobs and place the kernels in a bowl. Add the remaining ingredients, stir to combine, and chill the salsa in the refrigerator for 1 hour before serving.

YIELD:
1½ CUPS

ACTIVE TIME:
5 MINUTES

TOTAL TIME:
5 MINUTES

CILANTRO PESTO

1 cup fresh cilantro

1 garlic clove

¼ cup roasted and shelled sunflower seeds

¼ cup shredded queso enchilada

¼ cup extra-virgin olive oil

1 teaspoon fresh lemon juice

Salt and pepper, to taste

1   Place all of the ingredients in a food processor and blitz until they have emulsified.

2   Serve the pesto immediately or store in the refrigerator.

YIELD:
3 CUPS

ACTIVE TIME:
20 MINUTES

TOTAL TIME:
45 MINUTES

MOJO DE AJO

10 oz. garlic cloves, unpeeled

1 cup unsalted butter

2 tablespoons guajillo chile powder

2 tablespoons chopped fresh cilantro

Salt, to taste

1   Place the garlic cloves in a dry skillet and toast them over medium heat until lightly charred in spots, about 10 minutes, turning them as necessary. Remove the garlic from the pan and let it cool slightly. When the garlic is cool enough to handle, peel it and set it aside.

2   Place the butter in the skillet and melt it over medium heat. Add the garlic and cook until the butter begins to foam and brown slightly. Remove the pan from heat and let the mixture cool to room temperature.

3   Place the butter, garlic, guajillo powder, and cilantro in a blender and puree until smooth. Season the sauce with salt and either serve it immediately or store in the refrigerator.

COCKTAILS

Part of the reason for the taco's popularity is how easy it is to prepare, how accessible it is, and its ability to be comforting while also making the meal feel like an occasion, as though a celebration is taking place.

This last characteristic means that tacos go hand in hand with a cocktail, particularly one centered around the unique flavors offered by tequila and mezcal. Whether you're looking to stick to tradition and prepare a Margarita or Paloma, or want something a bit more elegant, these drinks provide a fitting cap to a memorable meal.

YIELD:
1 DRINK

ACTIVE TIME:
2 MINUTES

TOTAL TIME:
2 MINUTES

MARGARITA

Salt, for the rim

2 oz. silver tequila

½ oz. Cointreau

1 oz. fresh lime juice

½ oz. Simple Syrup (see page 241)

3 dashes of Saline Solution (see page 241)

1 lime wedge, for garnish

1   Wet the rim of a double rocks glass and rim half of it with salt.

2   Place the remaining ingredients, except for the garnish, in a cocktail shaker, fill it two-thirds of the way with ice, and shake until chilled.

3   Pour the contents of the shaker into the rimmed glass and add more ice if desired.

4   Garnish with the lime wedge and enjoy.

YIELD:
1 DRINK

ACTIVE TIME:
2 MINUTES

TOTAL TIME:
2 MINUTES

PLAYA ROSITA

¾ oz. reposado tequila

¾ oz. mezcal

½ oz. Pineapple-Infused Campari (see page 242)

½ oz. sweet vermouth

½ oz. dry vermouth

Dash of Bittermens 'Elemakule Tiki Bitters

1 orange twist, for garnish

1   Chill a cocktail glass in the freezer.

2   Place all of the ingredients, except for the garnish, in a mixing glass, fill it two-thirds of the way with ice, and stir until chilled.

3   Strain into the chilled cocktail glass, garnish with the orange twist, and enjoy.

YIELD:
1 DRINK

ACTIVE TIME:
2 MINUTES

TOTAL TIME:
2 MINUTES

. . . .

RAMON BRAVO

. . . .

Salt, for the rim

1½ oz. Chorizo-Washed Mezcal (see page 243)

½ oz. Ancho Reyes liqueur

1 oz. Charred Pineapple Puree (see page 244)

1 oz. fresh lime juice

¾ oz. Simple Syrup (see page 241)

4 sprigs of fresh cilantro

1   Wet the rim of a double rocks glass and rim it with salt.

2   Place all of the remaining ingredients in a cocktail shaker, fill it two-thirds of the way with ice, and shake until chilled.

3   Strain into the rimmed glass and enjoy.

YIELD:
1 DRINK

ACTIVE TIME:
2 MINUTES

TOTAL TIME:
2 MINUTES

VAMPIRO

Tajín, for the rim

2 oz. mezcal

**2 oz. Vampiro Mix
(see page 242)**

½ oz. fresh lime juice

2 oz. fresh grapefruit juice

**¾ oz. Simple Syrup
(see page 241)**

Pinch of kosher salt

2 oz. seltzer water

**1 dehydrated blood orange
wheel, for garnish**

1   Wet the rim of a Collins glass and rim half of it with tajín.

2   Place the mezcal, Vampiro Mix, juices, and syrup in a cocktail
shaker, add 1 ice cube, and shake until chilled.

3   Pour the contents of the shaker into the rimmed glass, add the salt
and seltzer, and gently stir to combine.

4   Add more ice if desired, garnish with the dehydrated blood orange
wheel, and enjoy.

VAMPIRO, SEE PAGE 173

YIELD:
1 DRINK

ACTIVE TIME:
2 MINUTES

TOTAL TIME:
2 MINUTES

. . . .

PALOMA

. . . .

Salt, for the rim

2 oz. silver tequila

1 oz. fresh grapefruit juice

½ oz. fresh lime juice

½ oz. Simple Syrup (see page 241)

2 oz. seltzer water

1 grapefruit slice, for garnish

1   Wet the rim of a Collins glass and coat it with salt.

2   Place the tequila, juices, and syrup in a cocktail shaker, add 1 or 2 ice cubes, and whip-shake until chilled.

3   Pour the contents of the shaker into the rimmed glass and top with the seltzer.

4   Add more ice to the glass, garnish with the grapefruit slice, and enjoy.

YIELD:
1 DRINK

ACTIVE TIME:
2 MINUTES

TOTAL TIME:
2 MINUTES

SPICY MARGARITA

Tajín, for the rim

2 oz. silver tequila

½ oz. Cointreau

1 oz. fresh lime juice

½ oz. Blistered Jalapeño Syrup (see page 243)

3 dashes of Saline Solution (see page 241)

1 lime wedge, for garnish

1   Wet the rim of a double rocks glass and rim half of it with tajín.

2   Place all of the ingredients, except for the garnish, in a cocktail shaker, fill it two-thirds of the way with ice, and shake until chilled.

3   Pour the contents of the shaker into the rimmed glass, and add ice, and garnish with the lime wedge.

YIELD:
1 DRINK

ACTIVE TIME:
2 MINUTES

TOTAL TIME:
2 MINUTES

BATANGA

2 pinches of kosher salt, plus more for the rim

½ oz. fresh lime juice

2 oz. silver tequila

3½ oz. Mexican Coca-Cola

1 lime wedge, for garnish

1 Wet the rim of a highball glass and rim it with salt.

2 Place the lime juice and salt in the glass and stir until the salt has dissolved.

3 Add the tequila and ice, top with the soda, and gently stir to combine.

4 Garnish with the lime wedge and enjoy.

YIELD:
1 DRINK

ACTIVE TIME:
2 MINUTES

TOTAL TIME:
2 MINUTES

ÚLTIMA PALABRA

¾ oz. mezcal

¾ oz. Green Chartreuse

¾ oz. Luxardo maraschino liqueur

¾ oz. fresh lime juice

1 Luxardo maraschino cherry, for garnish

1   Chill a coupe in the freezer.

2   Place all of the ingredients, except for the garnish, in a cocktail shaker, fill it two-thirds of the way with ice, and shake until chilled.

3   Double-strain into the chilled coupe, garnish with the maraschino cherry, and enjoy.

ÚLTIMA PALABRA, SEE PAGE 181

YIELD:
1 DRINK

ACTIVE TIME:
2 MINUTES

TOTAL TIME:
2 MINUTES

EAST LA

4 slices of cucumber, plus more for garnish

1 oz. fresh key lime juice

2 oz. silver tequila

¾ oz. Simple Syrup (see page 241)

8 fresh mint leaves

3 drops of Saline Solution (see page 241)

1   Place the cucumber and key lime juice in a cocktail shaker and muddle.

2   Add the tequila and syrup, give the mint leaves a smack, and drop them into the shaker. Fill the shaker two-thirds of the way with ice, add the Saline Solution, and shake until chilled.

3   Double-strain over ice into a rocks glass, garnish with an additional slice of cucumber, and enjoy.

YIELD:
1 DRINK

ACTIVE TIME:
2 MINUTES

TOTAL TIME:
2 MINUTES

RANCH WATER

Salt, for the rim, plus more to taste

2 oz. silver tequila

½ oz. fresh lime juice

4 oz. Topo Chico

1 lime wedge, for garnish

1   Wet the rim of a highball glass and rim it with salt. Add ice to the glass along with the tequila and lime juice.

2   Top with the Top Chico, add a pinch of salt, and gently stir.

3   Garnish with the lime wedge and enjoy.

YIELD:
1 DRINK

ACTIVE TIME:
2 MINUTES

TOTAL TIME:
2 MINUTES

OAXACA OLD FASHIONED

1½ oz. reposado tequila

½ oz. mezcal

2 dashes of Angostura Bitters

1 bar spoon of agave nectar

1 strip of orange peel, torched, for garnish

1 Place all of the ingredients, except for the garnish, in a mixing glass, fill it two-thirds of the way with ice, and stir until chilled.

2 Strain into a rocks glass, garnish with the torched orange peel, and enjoy.

YIELD:
1 DRINK

ACTIVE TIME:
2 MINUTES

TOTAL TIME:
2 MINUTES

EL CHAVO DEL OCHO

2 oz. silver tequila

½ oz. Licor 43

½ oz. fresh lime juice

¾ oz passion fruit puree

**½ oz. Thyme Syrup
(see page 244)**

1 egg white

**1 sprig of fresh thyme, for
garnish**

1   Place all of the ingredients, except for the garnish, in a cocktail shaker, add 1 ice cube, and whip-shake until chilled.

2   Strain into a large coupe or a wineglass, garnish with the fresh thyme, and enjoy.

YIELD:
1 DRINK

ACTIVE TIME:
2 MINUTES

TOTAL TIME:
2 MINUTES

OAXACARAJILLO

1½ oz. Licor 43

1 oz. mezcal

1 bar spoon of agave nectar

1 oz. freshly brewed espresso

1 Add the Licor 43, mezcal, and agave nectar to a double rocks glass.

2 Add 1 large ice cube. Slowly pour the espresso over the back of a bar spoon positioned as close to the cube as possible so that it floats atop the cocktail, and enjoy.

OAXACARAJILLO, SEE PAGE 191

YIELD:
1 DRINK

ACTIVE TIME:
2 MINUTES

TOTAL TIME:
2 MINUTES

CANOE CLUB

1½ oz. mezcal

½ oz. crème de mure

¾ oz. Ginger & Serrano
Syrup (see page 245)

½ oz. fresh lime juice

3 dashes of Peychaud's
Bitters

1   Place all of the ingredients in a cocktail shaker and stir to combine.
    Fill the shaker two-thirds of the way with ice and shake until chilled.

2   Strain over ice into a rocks glass and enjoy.

YIELD:
1 DRINK

ACTIVE TIME:
2 MINUTES

TOTAL TIME:
2 MINUTES

· ·

FLOR DE JALISCO

· ·

1½ oz. reposado tequila

½ oz. mezcal

½ oz. strawberry jam

½ oz. agave nectar

½ oz. fresh lime juice

Dash of Black Lava Solution (see page 246)

3 dashes of Bittermens Hellfire Habanero Shrub

2 pineapple leaves, for garnish

1 lime wheel, for garnish

1 marigold blossom, for garnish

1   Place all of the ingredients, except for the garnishes, in a cocktail shaker, fill it two-thirds of the way with ice, and shake until chilled.

2   Strain over ice into a rocks glass, garnish with the pineapple leaves, a lime wheel, and a marigold blossom, and enjoy.

YIELD:
1 DRINK

ACTIVE TIME:
2 MINUTES

TOTAL TIME:
2 MINUTES

LAVAGAVE

1½ oz. silver tequila

½ oz. mezcal

¾ oz. Lavender Agave
(see page 246)

½ oz. grapefruit juice

½ oz. fresh lime juice

¾ oz. egg white

Dash of Bittercube Cherry
Bark Vanilla Bitters

Dried lavender buds,
grated, for garnish

1   Chill a coupe in the freezer.

2   Place all of the ingredients, except for the garnish, in a cocktail shaker, fill it two-thirds of the way with ice, and shake until chilled.

3   Strain, discard the ice in the shaker, return the cocktail to the shaker, and dry shake for 15 seconds.

4   Pour the drink into the chilled coupe, garnish with grated lavender buds, and enjoy.

YIELD:
1 DRINK

ACTIVE TIME:
2 MINUTES

TOTAL TIME:
2 MINUTES

BLACKER THE BERRY, THE SWEETER THE JUICE

5 blackberries

1½ oz. mezcal

¾ oz. St-Germain

½ oz. Ginger Syrup (see page 247)

2 dashes of Bittermens Hellfire Habanero Shrub

¾ oz. fresh lime juice

½ oz. agave nectar

1 lime wheel, for garnish

2 fresh sage leaves, for garnish

1   Place blackberries in a highball glass and muddle them. Add crushed ice to the glass.

2   Place the mezcal, St-Germain, syrup, shrub, lime juice, and agave in a cocktail shaker, fill it two-thirds of the way with ice, and shake until chilled.

3   Strain into the highball glass, garnish with the lime wheel and fresh sage, and enjoy.

YIELD:
1 DRINK

ACTIVE TIME:
2 MINUTES

TOTAL TIME:
2 MINUTES

DRUNKEN RABBIT

2 oz. mezcal

1 oz. Ancho Reyes liqueur

1½ oz. pineapple juice

1½ oz. guava juice

1 oz. Cinnamon Syrup (see page 247)

Pineapple leaves, for garnish

1 pineapple chunk, for garnish

1   Place all of the ingredients, except for the garnishes, in a cocktail shaker, fill it two-thirds of the way with crushed ice, and shake until chilled.

2   Pour the contents of the shaker into a coupe, garnish with pineapple leaves and a pineapple chunk, and enjoy.

YIELD:
1 DRINK

ACTIVE TIME:
2 MINUTES

TOTAL TIME:
2 MINUTES

SHAKE YOUR TAMARIND

1½ oz. reposado tequila

¼ oz. mezcal

¼ oz. Campari

¾ oz. tamarind concentrate

¾ oz. Cinnamon Syrup (see page 247)

¼ oz. fresh lime juice

Fresh mint, for garnish

1 cinnamon stick, for garnish

1 lime wheel, for garnish

1   Place all of the ingredients, except for the garnishes, in a cocktail shaker, fill it two-thirds of the way with ice, and shake until chilled.

2   Double-strain over ice into a rocks glass, garnish with fresh mint, the cinnamon stick, and lime wheel, and enjoy.

YIELD:
1 DRINK

ACTIVE TIME:
2 MINUTES

TOTAL TIME:
2 MINUTES

THE FIFTH ELEMENT

Citrus Salt (see page 248), for the rim

2 oz. silver tequila

2 oz. Avocado Mix (see page 248)

¾ oz. fresh lime juice

½ oz. agave nectar

1 egg white

1 dehydrated lime slice, for garnish

1   Wet the rim of a coupe and rim it with the Citrus Salt.

2   Place all of the remaining ingredients, except for the garnish, in a cocktail shaker, fill it two-thirds of the way with ice, and shake until chilled.

3   Strain into the rimmed coupe, garnish with the dehydrated lime slice, and enjoy.

YIELD:
1 DRINK

ACTIVE TIME:
2 MINUTES

TOTAL TIME:
2 MINUTES

LA DIOSA

1½ oz. silver tequila

¾ oz. triple sec

½ oz. fresh lime juice

1 tablespoon Pineapple Marmalade (see page 249)

½ bar spoon of chili powder

1 small bunch of fresh cilantro

1 egg white

Edible flowers, for garnish

Tajín, for garnish

1   Place all of the ingredients, except for the egg white and garnishes, in a cocktail shaker, fill it two-thirds of the way with ice, and shake until chilled.

2   Strain, discard the ice, and return the mixture to the shaker. Add the egg white and dry shake for 15 seconds.

3   Strain into a coupe, garnish with the flowers and tajín, and enjoy.

YIELD:
1 DRINK

ACTIVE TIME:
2 MINUTES

TOTAL TIME:
2 MINUTES

QUINTANA ROO

1⅔ oz. silver tequila

1 oz. fresh tomato, chopped

⅔ oz. paprika

2 bar spoons of fresh lime juice

2 bar spoons of fresh lemon juice

Bar spoon of agave nectar

¼ teaspoon chili powder

Pinch of pink pepper

Dash of Bob's Coriander Bitters

1 strip of lime peel, for garnish

1   Place all of the ingredients, except for the garnish, in a blender and pulse until combined.

2   Strain the mixture into a cocktail shaker, fill it two-thirds of the way with ice, and shake until chilled.

3   Strain into a cocktail glass and garnish with the strip of lime peel.

YIELD:
1 DRINK

ACTIVE TIME:
2 MINUTES

TOTAL TIME:
2 MINUTES

MAYA GOLD

1½ oz. Chamomile Mezcal (see page 245)

¾ oz. fino sherry

½ oz. Aperol

½ oz. Yellow Chartreuse

1 lemon twist, for garnish

1   Chill a coupe in the freezer.

2   Place all of the ingredients, except for the garnish, in a mixing glass, fill it two-thirds of the way with ice, and stir until chilled.

3   Strain into the chilled coupe, garnish with the lemon twist, and enjoy.

MAYA GOLD, SEE PAGE 211

YIELD:
1 DRINK

ACTIVE TIME:
2 MINUTES

TOTAL TIME:
2 MINUTES

SUNDAY MORNING COMING DOWN

1⅜ oz. silver tequila

½ oz. dry vermouth

⅜ oz. Aperol

1 teaspoon agave nectar

5 drops of Bittermens Hellfire Habanero Shrub

1 strip of orange peel, for garnish

1 Chill a cocktail glass in the freezer.

2 Place all of the ingredients, except for the garnish, in a mixing glass and fill it two-thirds of the way with ice. Using another, empty mixing glass, pour the cocktail back and forth between the glasses until it is combined.

3 Strain over 2 ice cubes into the chilled cocktail glass. Express the strip of orange peel over the cocktail, garnish the drink with it, and enjoy.

YIELD:
1 DRINK

ACTIVE TIME:
2 MINUTES

TOTAL TIME:
2 MINUTES

SPARKLING PALOMA

Salt, for the rim

¾ oz. silver tequila

1¼ oz. pink grapefruit juice

1¼ oz. white grapefruit juice

Dash of Cinnamon Syrup (see page 247)

Champagne, to top

1 sprig of fresh rosemary, for garnish

1   Wet the rim of a wineglass and rim it with salt.

2   Place the tequila, juices, and syrup in a mixing glass, fill it two-thirds of the way with ice, and stir until chilled.

3   Strain into the rimmed glass and top with the Champagne.

4   Garnish with the fresh rosemary and enjoy.

SPARKLING PALOMA, SEE PAGE 215

YIELD:
1 DRINK

ACTIVE TIME:
2 MINUTES

TOTAL TIME:
2 MINUTES

LOST IN THE RAIN IN JUÁREZ

1 oz. mezcal

¾ oz. Aperol

⅞ oz. fresh lime juice

½ oz. Demerara Syrup
(see page 250)

1¼ oz. pineapple juice

3 dashes of absinthe

1 egg white

1 dehydrated pineapple
chunk, for garnish

1   Place all of the ingredients, except for the garnish, in a cocktail shaker and dry shake for 15 seconds.

2   Add ice and shake until chilled.

3   Double-strain into a coupe, garnish with the chunk of dehydrated pineapple, and enjoy.

YIELD:
1 DRINK

ACTIVE TIME:
2 MINUTES

TOTAL TIME:
2 MINUTES

PIÑA FUMADA

1¼ oz. mezcal

¾ oz. fresh lemon juice

2 teaspoons Velvet Falernum

½ oz. Honey Syrup (see page 250)

Club soda, to top

1 pineapple leaf, for garnish

1 lemon wedge, for garnish

1   Place all of the ingredients, except for the club soda and garnishes, in a cocktail shaker, fill it two-thirds of the way with ice, and shake until chilled.

2   Strain over crushed ice into a highball glass and top with the club soda.

3   Add more crushed ice, garnish with the pineapple leaf and lemon wedge, and enjoy.

DISCOUNT
SUIT
COMPANY

29a WENTWORTH
STREET E1 7TB

020 7247 8755

bookings@discount
suitcompany.co.uk

instagram.com/
discountsuitcompany

facebook.com/
discountsuitco

twitter.com/
discountsuitco

YIELD:
1 DRINK

ACTIVE TIME:
2 MINUTES

TOTAL TIME:
2 MINUTES

PICASSO

1¾ oz. mezcal

⅞ oz. Cocchi Americano

¾ oz. Lime Syrup (see page 251)

⅞ oz. fresh lemon juice

Absinthe, to mist

3 maraschino cherries, for garnish

1   Place the mezcal, Cocchi Americano, syrup, and lemon juice in a cocktail shaker, fill it two-thirds of the way with ice, and shake until chilled.

2   Strain into a cocktail glass and mist the cocktail with absinthe. Garnish with the maraschino cherries, speared on a toothpick, and enjoy.

YIELD:
1 DRINK

ACTIVE TIME:
2 MINUTES

TOTAL TIME:
2 MINUTES

. . . .

CANTARITOS

. . . .

2 oz. reposado tequila

1½ oz. fresh orange juice

¾ oz. fresh pink grapefruit juice

½ oz. fresh lime juice

2 pinches of fine sea salt

2 oz. pink grapefruit soda

1 lime wedge, for garnish

1   Build the cocktail in a clay jar or Collins glass filled with ice, adding all of the ingredients, except for the garnish, in the order they are listed.

2   Gently stir to combine, garnish with the lime wedge, and enjoy.

YIELD:
1 DRINK

ACTIVE TIME:
2 MINUTES

TOTAL TIME:
2 MINUTES

NAKED & FAMOUS

¾ oz. mezcal

¾ oz. Yellow Chartreuse

¾ oz. Aperol

¾ oz. fresh lime juice

1 Chill a coupe in the freezer.

2 Place all of the ingredients in a cocktail shaker, fill the shaker two-thirds of the way with ice, and shake until chilled.

3 Strain into the chilled coupe and enjoy.

YIELD:
1 DRINK

ACTIVE TIME:
2 MINUTES

TOTAL TIME:
2 MINUTES

. . . .

KINDA KNEW ANNA

. . . .

1 oz. silver tequila

1 oz. crème de mure

1 oz. fresh lime juice

2 oz. ginger beer

1 fresh sage leaf, for garnish

1   Place the tequila, crème de mure, and lime juice in a cocktail shaker, fill it two-thirds of the way with ice, and shake until chilled.

2   Strain over ice into a double rocks glass and top with the ginger beer.

3   Garnish with the sage leaf and enjoy.

YIELD:
1 DRINK

ACTIVE TIME:
2 MINUTES

TOTAL TIME:
2 MINUTES

JALISCO SOUR

1 oz. silver tequila

1 oz. pisco

¾ oz. fresh lime juice

**¾ oz. Simple Syrup
(see page 241)**

**3 dashes of Angostura
Bitters, for garnish**

1   Place all of the ingredients, except for the garnish, in a cocktail shaker, fill it two-thirds of the way with crushed ice, and shake until chilled.

2   Strain into a rocks glass, garnish with the bitters, and enjoy.

YIELD:
1 DRINK

ACTIVE TIME:
2 MINUTES

TOTAL TIME:
2 MINUTES

SHE'S A RAINBOW

2 oz. silver tequila

1 oz. Midori

5 oz. white grapefruit juice

1 grapefruit slice, for garnish

1 Place all of the ingredients, except for the garnish, in a cocktail shaker, fill it two-thirds of the way with ice, and shake until chilled.

2 Strain over ice into a highball glass, garnish with the slice of grapefruit, and enjoy.

YIELD:
1 DRINK

ACTIVE TIME:
2 MINUTES

TOTAL TIME:
2 MINUTES

TRUE ROMANCE

1½ oz. mezcal

1 oz. Yellow Chartreuse

¾ oz. Averna Amaro

1 lime twist, for garnish

Pinch of fine sea salt, for garnish

1   Place the mezcal, Chartreuse, and amaro in a rocks glass containing one large ice cube and stir until chilled.

2   Garnish with the lime twist and pinch of sea salt and enjoy.

YIELD:
1 DRINK

ACTIVE TIME:
2 MINUTES

TOTAL TIME:
2 MINUTES

FIRE WALK WITH ME

½ oz. fresh lime juice

½ oz. Orgeat (see page 251)

2 slices of jalapeño chile pepper

2 oz. reposado tequila

½ oz. Velvet Falernum

1 strip of orange peel, for garnish

1   Chill a coupe in the freezer.

2   Place the lime juice, Orgeat, and jalapeño in a cocktail shaker and muddle.

3   Add ice, the tequila, and falernum and shake until chilled.

4   Strain into the chilled coupe, garnish with the strip of orange peel, and enjoy.

APPENDIX

BIRRIA

5 lbs. beef chuck, cut into 3-inch cubes

10 guajillo chile peppers

1 teaspoon black peppercorns

½ cinnamon stick

1 tablespoon dried oregano

1 teaspoon allspice

½ teaspoon cumin

Salt, to taste

5 garlic cloves

2 tablespoons white vinegar

2 tablespoons extra-virgin olive oil

1 onion, finely diced

3 large tomatoes, diced

2 bay leaves

1   Place the beef in a baking dish and set it aside.

2   Place the guajillo peppers in a dry skillet and toast them over medium heat until they darken and become fragrant and pliable. Remove them from the pan, place them in a bowl of boiling water, and let them soak for 15 minutes.

3   Place the peppercorns and cinnamon stick in the dry skillet and toast until fragrant, shaking the pan frequently. Combine the toasted spices with the oregano, allspice, and cumin and grind the mixture into a fine powder with a mortar and pestle or a spice grinder.

4   Season the meat with salt and spice powder. Drain the guajillo peppers and place them in a blender along with the garlic and white vinegar. Puree until smooth and then rub the puree over the meat until it is coated. Marinate in the refrigerator overnight.

5   Remove the meat from the refrigerator an hour before you intend to cook.

6   Preheat the oven to 350°F. Place the olive oil in a Dutch oven and warm it over medium heat. Add the onion and cook, stirring occasionally, until it is translucent, about 3 minutes.

7   Stir in the tomatoes, bay leaves, meat, marinade, and 1 cup water and bring to a boil. Cover the pot, place it in the oven, and braise until the meat is very tender, about 3 hours. Check the meat every hour to make sure it has enough liquid. You don't want to skim off any of the fat, as this will remove liquid from the pot and flavor from the finished broth.

8   Remove the meat from the pot and shred the pieces that haven't fallen apart. Stir the meat back into the liquid and use as desired.

BEEF STOCK

2 lbs. yellow onions, chopped

1 lb. carrots, chopped

1 lb. celery, chopped

5 lbs. beef bones

2 tablespoons tomato paste

16 cups water

1 cup red wine

1 tablespoon black peppercorns

2 bay leaves

3 sprigs of fresh thyme

3 sprigs of fresh parsley

1   Preheat the oven to 375°F. Divide the onions, carrots, and celery among two baking sheets in even layers. Place the beef bones on top, place the pans in the oven, and roast the vegetables and beef bones for 45 minutes.

2   Spread the tomato paste over the beef bones and then roast for another 5 minutes.

3   Remove the pans from the oven, transfer the vegetables and beef bones to a stockpot, and cover with the water. Bring to a boil.

4   Reduce the heat so that the stock simmers. Deglaze the baking sheets with the red wine, scraping up any browned bits from the bottom. Stir the liquid into the stock, add the remaining ingredients, and cook, skimming any impurities that rise to the surface, until the stock has reduced by half and the flavor is to your liking, about 6 hours.

5   Strain the stock and either use immediately or let it cool completely before storing in the refrigerator.

RECADO ROJO

3½ oz. Yucateca achoite paste

14 tablespoons fresh lime juice

14 tablespoons orange juice

7 tablespoons grapefruit juice

1 teaspoon dried Mexican oregano

1 teaspoon dried marjoram

1 habanero chile pepper, stem and seeds removed

5 garlic cloves

1 cinnamon stick, grated

Salt, to taste

1   Place the achiote paste and juices in a bowl and let the mixture sit for 15 minutes.

2   Place the mixture and the remaining ingredients in a blender and puree until smooth.

3   Taste, adjust the seasoning as needed, and use as desired.

CHICKEN STOCK

5 lbs. chicken bones

32 cups cold water

¼ cup white wine

1 onion, chopped

1 celery stalk, chopped

1 carrot, chopped

2 bay leaves

10 sprigs of fresh parsley

10 sprigs of fresh thyme

1 teaspoon black peppercorns

Salt, to taste

1   Preheat the oven to 400°F. Place the chicken bones on a baking sheet, place them in the oven, and roast them until they are caramelized, about 1 hour.

2   Remove the chicken bones from the oven and place them in a stockpot. Cover them with the water and bring to a boil, skimming to remove any impurities that rise to the surface.

3   Deglaze the baking sheet with the white wine, scraping up any browned bits from the bottom. Stir the liquid into the stock, add the remaining ingredients, and reduce the heat so that the stock simmers. Simmer the stock until it has reduced by three-quarters and the flavor is to your liking, 6 to 8 hours, skimming the surface as needed.

4   Strain the stock and either use immediately or let it cool completely and store it in the refrigerator.

SIMPLE SYRUP

1 cup water

1 cup sugar

1   Place the water in a saucepan and bring it to a boil.

2   Add the sugar and stir until it has dissolved.

3   Remove the pan from heat and let the syrup cool before using or storing in the refrigerator, where it will keep for up to 3 months.

SALINE SOLUTION

1 oz. salt

Warm water, as needed

1   Place the salt in a mason jar and add warm water until the mixture measures 10 oz.

2   Stir to combine and let the solution cool before using or storing.

PINEAPPLE-INFUSED CAMPARI

¾ lb. pineapple, finely diced

1½ cups Campari

1 Place the ingredients in a large container and let the mixture steep for 24 to 48 hours.

2 Strain before using or storing in an airtight container.

VAMPIRO MIX

10 oz. Clamato

1 oz. apple cider vinegar

3 oz. fresh lime juice

2 oz. agave nectar

1 tablespoon sriracha

2 teaspoons blood orange juice

2 teaspoons smoked paprika

1 teaspoon black pepper

1 Place all of the ingredients in a blender and pulse until combined.

2 Use immediately or store in the refrigerator.

BLISTERED JALAPEÑO SYRUP

6 jalapeño chile peppers, stems and seeds removed, sliced

2 cups water

2 cups sugar

1 Warm a cast-iron skillet over medium heat. Add the jalapeños and cook until they are lightly charred, turning them occasionally.

2 Place the jalapeños in a blender, add the water and sugar, and puree on high for 30 seconds.

3 Strain before using or storing in the refrigerator.

CHORIZO-WASHED MEZCAL

½ lb. Mexican chorizo

Mezcal, as needed

1 Place the chorizo in a dry skillet and cook it over low heat to render the fat, stirring occasionally. When the chorizo is cooked through, remove it from the pan and use it in another preparation.

2 Place the rendered fat in a large mason jar. For every 2 oz. of fat, add a 750 ml bottle of mezcal. Let the mixture sit at room temperature for 12 hours.

3 Place the jar in the freezer for 6 to 8 hours.

4 Strain the mezcal through a fine sieve or cheesecloth and either use immediately or store it in an airtight container.

CHARRED PINEAPPLE PUREE

1 pineapple, peeled, cored, and sliced

Water, as needed

1   Prepare a gas or charcoal grill for medium heat (about 400°F). Place the pineapple on the grill and cook until it is charred on both sides, about 6 minutes.

2   Place the pineapple in a blender and pulse, adding water a tablespoon at a time until the texture of the puree is similar to applesauce. Use immediately or store in the refrigerator.

THYME SYRUP

1 cup water

1 cup sugar

6 sprigs of fresh thyme

1   Place the water in a saucepan and bring to a boil.

2   Add the sugar and thyme and stir until the sugar has dissolved.

3   Remove the pan from heat and let the syrup cool completely.

CHAMOMILE MEZCAL

¼ cup loose-leaf
chamomile tea

1 cup mezcal

1   Place the ingredients in a large mason jar and steep for 30 minutes to 1 hour, tasting the mixture every 5 minutes after the 30-minute mark to account for the varying results produced by different mezcals.

2   Strain before using or storing in an airtight container.

GINGER & SERRANO SYRUP

1 cup sugar

½ cup water

3 serrano chile peppers,
stems and seeds removed,
sliced

2 large pieces of fresh
ginger, chopped

1   Place all of the ingredients in a saucepan and bring to a boil, stirring to dissolve the sugar.

2   Remove the pan from heat and let the syrup cool completely.

3   Strain before using or storing in the refrigerator.

BLACK LAVA SOLUTION

½ cup water

¼ cup black lava salt

1 Place the ingredients in a saucepan and bring the mixture to a boil, stirring until the salt has dissolved.

2 Remove the pan from heat and let it cool completely before using or storing in an airtight container.

LAVENDER AGAVE

1 teaspoon dried lavender buds

4 cups agave nectar

1 Place the lavender buds in a piece of cheesecloth and use kitchen twine to fashion a sachet.

2 Place the agave in a saucepan and bring it to a simmer.

3 Remove the pan from heat, add the sachet to the agave, and let it steep for 2 hours.

4 Remove the sachet from the syrup before using or storing it in the refrigerator.

GINGER SYRUP

1 cup water

1 cup sugar

2-inch piece of fresh ginger, unpeeled and chopped

1 Place the water in a saucepan and bring it to a boil.

2 Add the sugar and stir until it has dissolved.

3 Stir in the ginger, remove the pan from heat, and let the syrup cool.

4 Strain the syrup before using or storing it in the refrigerator.

CINNAMON SYRUP

1 cup water

2 cinnamon sticks

2 cups sugar

1 Place the water and cinnamon sticks in a saucepan and bring the mixture to a boil.

2 Add the sugar and stir until it has dissolved. Remove the pan from heat.

3 Cover the pan and let the syrup sit at room temperature for 12 hours.

4 Strain the syrup before using or storing it in the refrigerator.

CITRUS SALT

Zest of 2 lemons

Zest of 2 limes

½ cup kosher salt

1   Combine all of the ingredients in a mixing bowl and either use immediately or store it in an airtight container.

AVOCADO MIX

Flesh of 3 avocados

2 lbs. pineapple, peeled and cored

¾ lb. fresh cilantro

1   Place all of the ingredients in a blender and puree until smooth.

2   Use immediately or store it in the refrigerator.

PINEAPPLE MARMALADE

4 pineapples, peeled, cored, and cubed

8 cinnamon sticks

¼ cup pure vanilla extract

4 orange peels

2 guajillo chile peppers, stems and seeds removed

1 cup sweet vermouth

1 cup Lillet

4 cups sugar

1   Place all of the ingredients in a large saucepan and bring to a simmer. Simmer for 5 hours, until the liquid has reduced by at least half.

2   Remove the cinnamon sticks and chiles. Place the remaining mixture in a blender and puree until smooth. Let the marmalade cool completely before using or storing in the refrigerator.

DEMERARA SYRUP

1 cup water

½ cup demerara sugar

1½ cups sugar

1   Place the water in a saucepan and bring it to a boil.

2   Add the sugars and stir until they have dissolved. Remove the pan from heat and let the syrup cool completely before using or storing.

HONEY SYRUP

1½ cups water

1½ cups honey

1   Place the water in a saucepan and bring it to a boil.

2   Add the honey and cook until it is just runny.

3   Remove the pan from heat and let the syrup cool completely before using or storing it in the refrigerator.

LIME SYRUP

2 cups Demerara Syrup
(see opposite page)

Zest of 3 limes

1 cup fresh lime juice

1 Place the syrup in a saucepan and warm it over medium-low heat.

2 Stir in the lime zest and lime juice and steep for 15 minutes.

3 Strain and let the syrup cool completely before using or storing in the refrigerator.

ORGEAT

2 cups almonds

1 cup Demerara Syrup (see opposite page)

1 teaspoon orange blossom water

1 teaspoon vodka

1 Preheat the oven to 400°F. Place the almonds on a baking sheet, place them in the oven, and toast until they are fragrant, about 5 minutes. Remove the almonds from the oven and let them cool completely.

2 Place the nuts in a food processor and pulse until they are a coarse meal. Set the almonds aside.

3 Place the syrup in a saucepan and warm it over medium heat. Add the almond meal, remove the pan from heat, and let the mixture steep for 6 hours.

4 Strain the mixture through cheesecloth and discard the solids. Stir in the orange blossom water and vodka. Use immediately or store the orgeat in the refrigerator.

METRIC CONVERSIONS

US Measurement	Approximate Metric Liquid Measurement	Approximate Metric Dry Measurement
1 teaspoon	5 ml	5 g
1 tablespoon or ½ ounce	15 ml	14 g
1 ounce or ⅛ cup	30 ml	29 g
¼ cup or 2 ounces	60 ml	57 g
⅓ cup	80 ml	76 g
½ cup or 4 ounces	120 ml	113 g
⅔ cup	160 ml	151 g
¾ cup or 6 ounces	180 ml	170 g
1 cup or 8 ounces or ½ pint	240 ml	227 g
1½ cups or 12 ounces	350 ml	340 g
2 cups or 1 pint or 16 ounces	475 ml	454 g
3 cups or 1½ pints	700 ml	680 g
4 cups or 2 pints or 1 quart	950 ml	908 g

INDEX

ABOUT CIDER MILL PRESS BOOK PUBLISHERS

Good ideas ripen with time. From seed to harvest, Cider Mill Press brings fine reading, information, and entertainment together between the covers of its creatively crafted books. Our Cider Mill bears fruit twice a year, publishing a new crop of titles each spring and fall.

"WHERE GOOD BOOKS ARE READY FOR PRESS"

501 Nelson Place

Nashville, Tennessee 37214

cidermillpress.com